Everyday Matters

Contemporary Approaches to Architecture

Edited by
Vanessa Grossman and Ciro Miguel

Ruby Press

Table of Contents

Foreword

Beatriz Colomina and Mark Wigley

Yes. Everyday matters.

Architectural discourse is captivated by the concept of the everyday in ways it can never fully articulate. It is hard to find architects for whom the everyday doesn't lurk as a reference point. Architects almost always point to overlooked routines, communities, protocols, systems, details, formats, technologies, or behaviors they have "found" and claim to be guided by or offer shelter to. The everyday is a kind of pre-architectural ready-made to be tweaked, protected, or magnified; to think, critique, teach, visualize, practice, or occupy architecture without seriously considering the everyday would be a kind of blindness. Yet the everyday is by definition blind. That which literally happens every day is so ever present, ever repeated, that it paradoxically goes unnoticed. The everyday is in this sense environmental, like water to fish—which is precisely what makes it so crucial to architects but also what torments them.

Most architectural discourse can even be understood as a form of resistance to the everyday it references. The very word cannot be spoken without perforating the conversation, ventilating architecture by opening it to its multiple others. Yet anything that is called everyday, and thereby brought into consciousness, is no longer everyday. One of the ways that architectural discourse resists the everyday is to point to it and thereby restrain it. After all, everyday life does not think of itself as everyday.

Although architects regularly describe themselves as offering hospitality to everyday acts, they rarely leave them untouched. The routine is no longer routine, especially when labelled "routine," "ordinary," "banal," "vernacular," "common," "local," or "domestic." The designers and theorists who elaborate a special respect for, even ambition toward, everydayness as a critique of the elitism of the field tend to patronize, colonize, and extract from what they celebrate. This extractive gesture shapes the field. The elitism of those who embrace the ordinary, or even embrace the extraordinary unrecognized "creativity" of the supposedly ordinary, is just as great as that of those who disdain it. And the ultimate patronizing gesture is to treat everydayness as a subaltern quality—as if those who are structurally disadvantaged, which is to say the vast majority, are condemned to the everyday—and to overlook the everydayness of privilege itself and the violence that sustains it.

This is not to criticize the politics of individual actors in architectural discourse, whether designers, clients, consultants, or critics. On the contrary, it is only to note that these complications and contradictions are built into the very concept of the everyday. The everyday is never simply "the" everyday, but multiplicities, clusters of seemingly incompatible, even antithetical conditions. The everyday is, for example, both alienation and authenticity, both the system (the unconscious repetitions that enslave those that repeat them and thereby enslave others) and the possibility of subverting the system. Architects reach for the everyday in both spirits—but only reach for, since the everyday by definition cannot be grasped, seen, or even named. The word points to the limits of architectural discourse, the limits that don't simply lie at the edge of the discourse but shape it, the limits that are, in that sense, the very basis, the foundations for the discourse. Nothing could be more urgent than to permanently reconsider the architecture of the everyday, the everyday in architecture, the architecture in the everyday, and everyday architecture—these being vastly different things that interact in complex ways.

Such an urgent project does more than pull architectural discourse into the present by uncovering its array of blind spots and fostering new senses of responsibility, agency, and activism. The work is also historical. After all, the concept of the everyday has a history, many histories, having been so intimately tied to political struggle over the last 150 years. It is neither singular nor static. It changes. Yet part of this change is to recognize appeals to the everyday in ancient, seemingly distant, overlooked texts, or to reconsider which texts, objects, spaces, and practices are architectural. To say it the other way around, rethinking the everyday is to rethink history. It is an opportunity for the discourse to undergo transformative self-analysis. It's a call for change. At the very least, it is a way to destabilize the routines of the field, which especially includes any by now habitual references to the everyday, any assumption that formulaic appeals to the everyday are progressive.

In this spirit, it might be helpful to recall Guy Debord's contribution to a May 1961 meeting of Henri Lefebvre's Group for Research on Everyday Life, presented via a tape recording, in which he considered the use of concepts like the everyday and the risks of treating the everyday as a colony to be mined by specialists, even if in the name of revolution. The talk begins by insisting that "to study everyday life would be a completely absurd undertaking, unable even to grasp anything of its object, if this study was not expressly for the purpose of transforming everyday life." Debord then immediately turns the tables by pointing out that everyday life was right there in the meeting itself, in the concepts, room, speaker–audience hierarchy, and communication media. If reflections on the everyday need to transform the everyday, there always has to be an “alteration” that starts, as it were, in the specialist’s home. The discourse itself has to continually break its conscious and unconscious routines. In resolutely refusing any singular or static understanding of the everyday, *Everyday Matters* offers itself as an invaluable tool for breaking and reentering architectural discourse.

Ester Carro, "Before," *Contributions to Another Narrative*, 2019

Everyday Matters

Vanessa Grossman and Ciro Miguel

Ms. Nilda and her five children used to suffer daily from roof leaks and a lack of space, light, and ventilation in their home in Jardim Colombo, a poor neighborhood in the western district of São Paulo. The house, built without any technical assistance, subsequently underwent a modest yet effective renovation led by Ester Carro, a Black architect who was born and raised only a few blocks from Ms. Nilda. Starting with low-tech construction solutions and standard building materials and components, new windows were opened, the floor was changed, the bathroom was slightly enlarged, and a new sink was installed; previously, owing to lack of space, the toilet was beneath the showerhead. The work radically affected the family's life.

When the subtle operations of repair and care proposed by Ester Carro for her community were gradually replicated across Jardim Colombo, they led to the conversion, with the assistance of Carro's design expertise, of an illegal landfill into a park for the neighborhood, which previously had no meeting or leisure area. The renovation of Ms. Nilda's house is not the kind of project that would offer an architect visibility or make headlines. Yet, by establishing a new relationship to resources, maintenance, community, and social life, the reputation of the intervention,

Ester Carro, "After," *Contributions to Another Narrative*, 2019

which Carro refers to as *Contributions to Another Narrative*, grew beyond the neighborhood's borders.[1] It epitomizes the potential of architecture to respond to global societal shifts that have become more evident in recent years. While most architects work on small houses, extensions, renovations, and retail fit outs, Carro's architecture deals with everyday issues in relation to structural societal change. Behind a mere house remodel lies a social project focused on equality and environmental justice.

Since the 2010s, efforts bouncing across different disciplines have reinforced the connection between architecture and everyday life. The relationship of humans to nonhumans, banal objects, and all sorts of routine maintenance protocols that constitute the daily life of the built environment have come to the forefront of architectural discourse and practice. Many architects now consider these to be the fundamental questions for their field, well beyond the built form that architectural plans have historically called for. In what could translate into an economy of means and material, these modes of intervention are not evidence of idleness or a lack of will; rather, they are geared toward making architecture a shared resort. Ultimately, they seek disciplinary legitimacy in a world that seems to have reached an unsustainable, overbuilt capacity, but where millions are still homeless and lack access to the most basic infrastructure. From research-based critical spatial practices to hands-on roles, what underlies these recent investments to reimagine the grounds of architecture, this book argues, is the concept of everyday life. The everyday has permeated architecture in the past, but in the last decade it has triggered the rise of a new ethics and aesthetics.

The Everyday in Other Days

In spite of its overarching meaning, which conflates temporal and spatial experience, the concept of everyday life remains tangible, and is found throughout the history of architecture and modernity.[2] Its elaboration within architecture, design, and planning has been largely fueled by these disciplines' intersections with politics, art, literature, and philosophy. In fact, the way the everyday has emerged in these fields as a critical construct can be traced back to the second half of the nineteenth century, a time when the modern idea of design and architecture was born. This idea is related to the vicissitudes of the dramatic acceleration of capitalist industrialization and urbanization in the then soon-to-be developed world, which drew heavily on the colonization of a still developing periphery. The emergence of the concept of the everyday can first be linked to the Paris Commune of 1871, where the social struggle of the newly routinized urban working class called for the political and revolutionary potential of what Kristin Ross has defined as the aesthetic reinvention of everyday life.[3] The Communards' claims extended well beyond holding political power to creative decisions embedded in every aspect of daily urban life, including a sense of festivity and the construction of a revolutionary urban space. The Commune's political, aesthetic, and urban imaginary was an important point of reference not only for contemporary supporters such as Karl Marx and William Morris but also for the architecture, design, and other artistic manifestations of modernism set forth by the historical avant-gardes of the first half of the twentieth century. Their core agenda for an aesthetic revolution of everyday life relied on the new cultural possibilities entailed by technology, mass production, and urban space.

For Vladimir Tatlin, for example, the 1917 October Revolution started from the most ordinary domestic confines to then shape the city of an urban-industrial future. With aim of reinventing the *byt* (everyday life) of the ideal socialist citizen, Tatlin and his architecture students designed mundane stoves and pots and pans for proletarian kitchens that would emancipate women.[4] According to the art theorist John Roberts, "The very connotations of *byt*—in Russian it signifies something hard, intractable, something that presses down relentlessly on the senses—become a material and moral virtue, the imposing and necessary industrial matter that needs to be molded and rebuilt."[5] After the Second World War, when modern architecture transitioned from the avant-garde to the technocratic establishment and the failure of a revolutionary program became evident in both the Soviet and the capitalist worlds—in view of unequal processes of urbanization, commodification, and consumption—the everyday transformed into what Mark Cousins referred to as a "postwar category."[6] In the 1940s, from the perspective of the developed world, Marxist philosopher and sociologist Henri Lefebvre began his pioneering theorizing of the mass production of urban space through what he called a "critique of everyday life," which resonated with the writings and experiments of Marxist-inflected postwar avant-garde formations like the Situationists and gradually gained enormous currency among architects.[7]

But the everyday also served as a critical lens on modernism's indulgences in Western consumer culture. In the 1950s, British architects Alison and Peter Smithson called, in texts and designs, for a conciliation of modern architecture with the "ugly" and the ordinary of the man in the street, searching for deep cultural meanings beyond the high-and-low modernist divide. From a transatlantic perspective, architect Denise Scott Brown began with the South African vernacular of improvised spaces and objects—standing well outside the tropes of industrialization and consumption—but after moving to the United States, together with Robert Venturi she pushed the Smithsons' assertion of the everyday as a critical inflection point for architectural modernism even further. Concerned with architecture's loss of symbolic meaning, Scott Brown and Venturi indulged in a democratization of taste through seminal books and buildings that came to subsidize the onslaught of postmodernism.

Moving south of the equator, from the perspective of the developing world, Italian-born Brazilian architect Lina Bo Bardi turned to banal things produced on the fringes of capitalism in Brazil's northeast, where consumer culture was (and still is) outside the reach of many. Familiar with Antonio Gramsci's theory of cultural hegemony, in the 1960s Bo Bardi began articulating the idea of "stalemate design," which she believed could reorient modernism to address the country's rough reality and people's everyday needs.[8] She designed objects and buildings to extol material improvisation and reuse, cultural inclusiveness and communitarianism.[9]

From that decade on, the concept of the everyday also fed the emergence of a grassroots counterculture of racial, gender, and ecological activism that developed beyond the Western world, what John Roberts calls "the arrival of a subaltern consciousness of the everyday."[10] Adding complexity to analyses of the entanglements of capitalism with building and spatial practices and social and environmental justice, this movement addressed themes ranging from decolonization and racial and gender apartheid to genocide and biological annihilation. For example, inspired by architect and systems theorist Buckminster Fuller—whose lifelong obsession was to optimize the earth's resources by "doing more with less"—the early tenets of the "everyday environmentalism" of publications such as the *Whole Earth Catalog* (1968–72) prompted a vision that deflected from institutions in favor of ecologically conscious individual empowerment. In the 1975 essay by Marxist-feminist theorists Nicole Cox and Silvia Federici entitled "Counter-planning from the Kitchen," the ordinary kitchen space emerged once more as a revolutionary point of departure for feminist anti-capitalist struggle. The notion of everyday life served to mediate this pioneering conflation of body and domesticity in feminist theory and art. Eventually, it even expanded the understanding of the political dimension of the domestic sphere: while daily life at home for most white European or American feminists was representative of subjugation, the family and community were important sites of anti-racist practices for many African American women.[11]

From the Paris Commune and Marx to thinkers interested in urban and domestic space like Henri Lefebvre, Michel de Certeau, and Milton Santos, from architects like Alison and Peter Smithson, Denise Scott Brown and Robert Venturi, and Lina Bo Bardi to trailblazing feminists like Nicole Cox and Silvia Federici and civil-rights activists and environmentalists, the notion of everyday life has been theoretically and aesthetically reframed over the last 150 years in view of capitalist developments that have reached new heights in the twenty-first century.

Today's Everyday Matters

German historian Reinhart Koselleck claims that the experience of the new is only possible if there are structures of repetition within the chaotic stream of events that we call history.[12] After its iterations throughout the twentieth century, the everyday has reemerged in the last decade, fueling new directions for contemporary architectural discourses and practices. These moves coincide with the biggest economic crisis in a half century. The downturn of the construction industry, among others, caused by the real estate crash at the center of the 2008 recession was only temporary. Yet the deep sense of social injustice and income inequality, which were both revealed and aggravated by the crash, persisted well beyond the economic recovery. In 2011, Occupy Wall Street and the Arab Spring reinvested the relation between politics, architecture, and virtual and urban everyday spaces; various thinkers have compared these activist movements to the Paris Commune.[13] Such movements gradually gained a new dimension when the socioeconomic upheaval began to be conflated with an upheaval of an even greater order involving all corners of the planet: in 2008, during the economic crash, the Stratigraphy Commission of the Geological Society in London considered a proposal to formally name the most recent geological epoch the Anthropocene. The term was first used in 2000 by chemist Paul Crutzen and ecologist Eugene Stoermer to define an age in which humans are modifying the earth more than the planet's natural processes.

An outcome of the recognition of the Anthropocene is that architects are being put on the front lines of climate change—they are commissioned to design flood-prone buildings and infrastructure, replace houses destroyed by mega-fires, and contribute to evacuation and accommodation plans to manage ongoing climate-related mass migrations.[14] As anthropologist Renzo Taddei reminds us in this book, the most distinctive quality of the Holocene (the geological age preceding the Anthropocene) was that the variation in climatic patterns was more stable than in previous epochs: "This exceptional level of stability greatly affected human production; everything that we call civilization, philosophy, politics, and religion was created during the Holocene." Humans are now considered a geological force, driven by technologies such as design, planning, and infrastructure. How, then, can unprecedented climate instability affect human culture, particularly a profession historically based on growth and modernization like architecture? In spite of past war-related traumas, including the fear of nuclear catastrophe, none of the predecessors of today's architects worried about the consequences of human activity on Earth as a whole. The image of *Anthropogenic Earth*, depicting soil depletion, wasteland zones, melting ice caps, and toxic clouds, transformed the forecasting of the countercultural ecology of the 1960s into a fait accompli.[15] The question is no longer of ecology but of survival, considering that many Indigenous peoples have already experienced the "end of their worlds."[16] The concept of the Anthropocene also poses questions of accountability: wealthy countries have caused 80 percent of all carbon-dioxide emissions since 1751, whereas the poorest countries have caused less than 1 percent.[17] The Anthropocene brought the notion of climate justice to the 2011 spatio-political arena that shed light on the share of the world's income captured by the top 1 percent.

Instead of fleeing the profession after 2008 for fear of a lack of work,[18] a generation of architects led a paradigm shift by seizing the opportunity to deploy new organizational, operational, and thematic grounds that constitute the framework this book calls "everyday matters." Embracing uncertainty, these architects drifted away from a world of infinite resources in both their professional output and means; they may seem limited in their ambit, but the intended outreach is not. If the impact of the discipline on the planet was to be reweighed, the footprint of even their own practices had to be reconsidered for the purpose of optimizing resources. Collaborative labor practices in architecture, such as collectives, ateliers, and cooperatives, have been reappraised and taken precedence. As architect Anna Heringer puts it in her contribution to this book, "I have been assessing my own level of sustainability, translating design into a joint effort with others." The newness of these less authorial labor arrangements lies in their reliance on the network paradigm facilitated by the internet and, for some, triggered by the ideas of Bruno Latour, a philosopher, anthropologist, and sociologist who has also collaborated with architects.[19] Chains of collaboration are established that are physical or virtual, or both, as well as interdisciplinary, involving peers, professionals from other disciplines, communities, and institution—often in a tussle of local versus global. Furthermore, such collective endeavors relate to issues of diversity and inclusiveness that impact architectural historians, including the notion of "global awareness," and foreground the role of things, materials, technologies, artificial intelligence, and other forms of automation and beings, which, as Latour has shown with his analysis of pasteurization, are not new.[20]

The professional scope of architects has also gone beyond building practices to include digital outputs like film, social media, mapping, forensics, and activism. Architect Markus Miessen argues in this book that there has been "a huge increase in the methods and protocols with which architects and urbanists have attempted to participate in (geo)-political spatial conditions that were not previously considered part of their job description." In 2010, an exhibition at New York's Museum of Modern Art entitled *Small Scale, Big Change: New Architectures of Social Engagement*, curated by architectural historian Andres Lepik, sought to grasp the "dramatic reevaluation" of architectural approaches committed to what the show called "radical pragmatism."[21] It showcased the "never demolish" retrofitting principles for France's *grands ensembles* by architects Anne Lacaton and Jean-Philippe Vassal as well as "Internet-based architecture communities" grounded in the idea that architecture's social responsibility can be facilitated by the digital. From 2010 until now, these pragmatic approaches have expanded the intricacies between the everyday and mass consumerist culture by tackling the planet's own consumption, or "broken world thinking,"[22] as information theorist Steven J. Jackson has written.

The implication is a reappraisal of the ordinary, because the ordinary is itself related to social phenomena, even if it does not have the heritage value of France's social housing claimed by Lacaton and Vassal. Representative of an attitude that reinforces the links between democratization and cultural production is the work of German architect Arno Brandlhuber. One of his projects was the reuse of the concrete towers of a factory in former East Berlin that survived the site's bulldozing because their demolition was too costly. With "little effort and intervention," Brandlhuber regulated the fire-safety and energy requirements of the high-rises for their new program as a production facility for architectural prototypes.[23] Brandlhuber's approach is in line with that of Brazilian architect Ester Carro and Mouraria 53, an interdisciplinary collective in Salvador for whom the "city is a quarry," as they state in their contribution here.

In ethos and substance, these approaches ultimately respond to cultural geographer Caitlin DeSilvey's provocation to the conventional thinking about heritage conservation. In her essay here, she reminds us of the urge for an "ethical stance that allows us to collaborate with—rather than defend against—natural processes." In a post-pandemic global scenario pointing to the fragility of the geopolitical, technical, and natural

Brandlhuber+ Georg Diez,
Nikolai von Rosen, and Christopher Roth,
San Gimignano Lichtenberg, Berlin, 2012–ongoing

worlds, the notions of everyday maintenance, care, and repair are becoming architecture's new mantra.[24] Architecture's turn to daily rituals of care and repair, either manual or automated, is fundamentally sociopolitical, as it brings to the fore the role and vulnerable status within capitalism of those who engage with the maintenance of the built environment and the very "natural processes" evoked by DeSilvey—poor workers, most of them women of color, Indigenous peoples, immigrants, and "global care chains" often moving from South to North.[25]

Portuguese architect Álvaro Siza once said that for him a house is "a complicated machine, in which every day something breaks down."[26] But who repairs it? This aspect of maintenance has hitherto seldomly been acknowledged by architects, or even in architectural history.[27] Think of the "Gremlin Grange" presented at the 1951 Festival of Britain Live: a full-size sectional demonstration of an interwar jerry-built semidetached house that featured structural cracks and leaning walls, deteriorating external plaster, damp walls, dangerously leaning chimney stacks, a leaking water tank, internal fissures in the walls, and bad artificial lighting. The crumbling pavilion was designed by architect John Ratcliff, the festival's deputy director of architecture, and was meant to show how many things could go wrong "when scientific principles in building were ignored."[28] Some architects are now questioning these "scientific principles" that were formerly taken for granted, even those allegedly addressing the environment, such as sustainability labels, by scrutinizing processes of construction and upkeep. Some have even started investigating a long-overlooked division of labor in architecture, also concerned with the conditions under which the control of maintenance protocols, services, and supplies becomes a weapon of hegemonic elites against supposedly subaltern professions, those who make sure architecture, infrastructure, the city, and nature are regularly taken care of: housekeepers, janitors, handymen, and handywomen. Subjugated in an exploitative situation, these are often the first to suffer from the lack of maintenance, living in communities situated at the margins of the economy, social-welfare systems, and public infrastructure.

For the project of a school prototype in Amazonas, architects Thiago Benucci and Daniel Jabra, together with members of the Yanomami, ancestral caretakers of the Amazon rainforest, decided that durable materials should be used in order to avoid the high maintenance costs of materials such as wood and straw that rot quickly in the tropical forest. Contrary to the architects' expectations of using traditional construction techniques, the project employed concrete, standardized wood, and plastic recycled roof tiles, that is, "white men's materials" that are not always at the disposal of the Yanomami. The architects' Yanomami interlocutors explained that "the school inside [their] territory could be built with materials from outside, the roof and the walls could be different, which would not mean that [they, the Yanomami] were going to change."[29] The criticism of modern materials and globalized products such as concrete, which looms large in recent inquiries of maintenance and sustainability, hardly appear to be burning issues to those who usually cannot access them. The Yanomami operate in what anthropologist James Ferguson calls the global shadows, which, in their case, lie beneath Amazonia's magnanimous canopies.[30] The satellite image of Earth at night, the so-called black marble, is the literal translation of Ferguson's thesis: the Yanomami settlement is a zone in darkness, a gap in the light map of the all-connected globalized world, "invisible in plain sight."[31] From different sides of the Atlantic, Brazilian philosopher Djamila Ribeiro and South African architects Ilze and Heinrich Wolff inquire, in this book, into the invisibility taking place in everyday spaces against the backdrop of systems of domination that perpetuate discrimination, pointing to the repair of communities and their physical and cultural survival.

Hence, from São Paulo and Rio to Cape Town, Madrid, New York, and beyond, architects are reflecting on the role of architecture while considering prospects linked to the production of space that range from the poetic subtleties of the quotidian to the revelation of the potentialities, violence, and inequalities that affect lives daily in the era of climate change. Architects are rethinking epistemic and aesthetic engagements with social and natural life;[32] raising awareness about the impact of technologies of resource extraction in urban, suburban, rural, and Indigenous contexts, from raw materials to the production and consumption of building components; inquiring about food and the provision of other daily resources and commodities such as water and electricity; and emphasizing the maintenance and care of the human body, domestic interiors, buildings, the city, and the planet at large—a long-overlooked subject. This new sensibility to issues of maintenance, which is being manifested both technically and aesthetically, has not only been triggered by the systemic and oppressive neglect that affects subjugated peoples worldwide. It is also embedded in the most recent catastrophes, climate-induced or not, that are compromising monuments, buildings, public institutions, and infrastructures in allegedly developed and underdeveloped worlds. The political disregard toward these social spaces and sites of collective memory exposes the materiality and fragility of architecture, which, despite advances in technology, is still highly dependent on the everyday care of humans.[33] Even the aforementioned tallest skyscrapers in the world, architectural and engineering

Atlantic rainforest, 2021. Photo by Pedro Kok

Yanomami community from the Upper Maraui river region together with architects Daniel Jabra and Thiago Benucci, Omaw Yanomami Differentiated Indigenous State School, Pukima Cachoeira community, Yanomami Indigenous land, Amazonas, Brazil, 2020

milestones, literal "high places" of the most immaterial wealth—that of financial capital—suffer from "creaks, leaks, and breaks."[34]

"Everyday matters" is what we call the conceptual framework that refers to the ideas and themes through which architects organize these new interventions. Everyday matters also refers to the architects' questioning of the means through which architecture should add to the materiality of the built environment, and therefore of the urge for design to critically take shape in both the Anthropocene and "the age of the thingless medium, the Internet."[35] If even the internet is only possible through buildings and massive infrastructure (from technical facilities to submarine cables hyperconnecting countries), what is the actual status of architecture as a building practice? By inquiring into these modes of exploration and the politics forged through them, this book seeks to expand contemporary notions of architecture. Additionally, to come to terms with the divide within culture—the natural and social aspects, to take a cue from Latour—this book offers accounts from the fields of anthropology, sociology of science and technology, cultural geography, history, and philosophy. The purpose is to convey a broader sense of the intellectual backdrop, methodological prerogatives, and affections that inform the architectural projects and reflections presented here, and the urgency we believe they share.

1 The project was presented under this title at Centro Cultural São Paulo as part of *Todo dia/Everyday*, the 12th International Architecture Biennale of São Paulo (September–December 2019), which was curated by the authors and Charlotte Malterre-Barthes.

2 A selection of recent reflections on the history of the everyday in architecture includes Steven Harris and Deborah Berke, eds., *Architecture of the Everyday* (New York: Princeton Architectural Press, 1997); John Chase, Margaret Crawford, and John Kaliski, eds., *Everyday Urbanism* (New York: Monacelli Press, 1999); "The Everyday," special issue, *Daidalos*, no. 75 (May 2000); Dirk van den Heuvel, "As Found: The Metamorphosis of the Everyday; On the Work of Nigel Henderson, Eduardo Paolozzi, and Alison and Peter Smithson (1953–1956)," *Oase*, no. 59 (2002): 52–67; Vanessa Grossman, *A arquitetura e o urbanismo revisitados pela Internacional Situacionista* (São Paulo: Annablume/FAPESP, 2006); Ricardo Agarez and Nelson Mota, "Architecture in Everyday Life," in "The 'Bread & Butter' of Architecture," special issue, *Footprint*, no. 17 (Autumn/Winter 2015): 1–8; Enrique Walker, *The Ordinary: Recordings* (New York: Columbia Books on Architecture and the City, 2018); and Jesús Vassallo, *Epics in the Everyday: Photography, Architecture, and the Problem of Realism* (Zurich: Park Books, 2020).

3 See Kristin Ross, *Communal Luxury: The Political Imaginary of the Paris Commune* (London: Verso, 2016).

4 See Laurel Fredrickson, "Vision and Material Practice: Vladimir Tatlin and the Design of Everyday Objects," *Design Issues* 15, no. 1 (Spring 1999): 49–74.

5 John Roberts, *Philosophizing the Everyday: Revolutionary Praxis and the Fate of Cultural Theory* (London: Pluto Press, 2006), 20.

6 Mark Cousins, "Where Is Everyday Life? Part I," AA School of

Architecture, London, October 12, 2012, video, 56:52, https://youtu.be/J_dxsa0Mkv4.

7 See Henri Lefebvre, *Critique de la vie quotidienne I* (Paris: L'Arche, 1958), 29. For the English translation, see Henri Lefebvre, *Critique of Everyday Life: The One-Volume Edition*, trans. John Moore (London: Verso, 2014). As Łukasz Stanek has shown, Lefebvre's theories also translated into a more direct involvement in urban planning and architecture. See Łukasz Stanek, *Henri Lefebvre on Space: Architecture, Urban Research, and the Production of Theory* (Minneapolis: University of Minnesota Press, 2011).

8 Lina Bo Bardi, *Tempos de grossura: O design no impasse* (São Paulo: Instituto Lina Bo e P.M. Bardi, 1994).

9 See Zeuler R. M. de A. Lima, "Lina Bo Bardi and the Architecture of Everyday Culture," *Places Journal*, November 2013, https://doi.org/10.22269/131112.

10 Roberts, *Philosophizing the Everyday*, 120.

11 See Barbara Smith, ed., *Home Girls: A Black Feminist Anthology* (New Brunswick, NJ: Rutgers University Press, 2000), cited in Simona de Simoni, "'Everyday Life': A Feminist Analysis," *Viewpoint Magazine*, February 12, 2015, https://viewpointmag.com/2015/02/12/everyday-life-a-feminist-analysis/.

12 See Reinhart Koselleck, *Sediments of Time: On Possible Histories*, ed. and trans. Sean Franzel and Stefan-Ludwig Hoffmann (Stanford, CA: Stanford University Press, 2018).

13 On the correlation between Occupy Wall Street and the Paris Commune, see Ross, *Communal Luxury*; and Noam Chomsky interviewed by Chris Steele, MIT,

Cambridge, MA, May 22, 2012, video, 3:46, https://www.youtube.com/watch?v=ajV9xoKWOL8. See also "The Paris Commune and the World," special issue, *Funambulist*, no. 34 (March–April 2021). Dedicated to the 150th anniversary of the Paris Commune, this issue includes articles that address connections between the commune and the Global South from 1871 to today.

14 See Dina Ionesco, Daria Mokhnacheva, and François Gemenne, *The Atlas of Environmental Migration* (London: Routledge, 2017).

15 See Alexandra Arènes, *Anthropogenic Earth* (2015), in Bruno Latour, "Can We Land on Earth?," interview by Line Marie Thorsen and Anette Vandsø, 153, http://s-o-c.fr/wp-content/uploads/2017/07/Can-we-land-on-earth.pdf.

16 Eduardo Viveiros de Castro,"Últimas notícias sobre a destruição do mundo," Centro de Estudos Ameríndios, Universidade de São Paulo, December 6, 2013, video, 1:49:54, https://www.youtube.com/watch?v=4BS4BO59yro.

17 Ian Angus, "Does Anthropocene Science Blame All Humanity?," *Climate & Capitalism*, May 31, 2015, https://climateandcapitalism.com/2015/05/31/does-anthropocene-science-blame-all-humanity/.

18 In a climacteric article, Nicolai Ouroussoff anticipated that "aspiring architects who [were] just emerging from graduate programs [were] likely to move on to more secure professions, which could spell a smaller talent pool in the future." Nicolai Ouroussoff, "Architecture Deluxe and Delusional: An Era Ends," *New York Times*, November 25,

2008, https://www.nytimes.com/2008/12/26/arts/26iht-architects.1.18918195.html.

19 Ava Kofman, "Bruno Latour, the Post-Truth Philosopher, Mounts a Defense of Science," *New York Times Magazine*, October 25, 2018, https://www.nytimes.com/2018/10/25/magazine/bruno-latour-post-truth-philosopher-science.html.

20 See Bruno Latour, *The Pasteurization of France*, trans. Alan Sheridan and John Law (Cambridge, MA: Harvard University Press, 1988).

21 See "Small Scale, Big Change: New Architectures of Social Engagement," MoMA, October 3, 2010–January 3, 2011, https://www.moma.org/calendar/exhibitions/1061.

22 Steven J. Jackson, "Rethinking Repair," in *Media Technologies: Essays on Communication, Materiality, and Society*, ed. Tarleton Gillespie, Pablo J. Boczkowski, and Kirsten A. Foot (Cambridge, MA: MIT Press, 2014), 221.

23 "San Gimignano Lichtenberg," Brandlhuber+, accessed March 3, 2021, https://bplus.xyz/projects/0154-san-gimignano-lichtenberg.

24 See Shannon Mattern, "Maintenance and Care," *Places Journal*, November 2018, https://doi.org/10.22269/181120.

25 Arlie Russell Hochschild, "Global Care Chains and Emotional Surplus Value," in *On the Edge: Living with Global Capitalism*, ed. Will Hutton and Anthony Giddens (London: Jonathan Cape, 2000), 130–46.

26 Álvaro Siza, "Living in a House" (1994), in Kenneth Frampton, *Álvaro Siza: Complete Works* (London: Phaidon, 2000), 252.

27 Influential books that address maintenance as a topic in the

discipline mostly focus on artistic practices; see, for example, Hilary Sample, *Maintenance Architecture* (Cambridge, MA: MIT Press, 2016).

28 Harding McGregor Dunnett, *1951 Exhibition of Architecture: Guide to the Exhibition of Architecture, Town Planning and Building Research* (London: Routledge, 2017), 32.

29 Daniel Jabra and Thiago Benucci, *Instrução para a construção de escolas indígenas diferenciadas nas comunidades yanomami do Rio Marauiá, Santa Isabel do Rio Negro – Documento yama siki taprarema hiramotima nahi pë rë upramamouwei xapono pë hami Komixipiwei u hami, Santa Isabel do Rio Negro urihi hami* (Santa Isabel do Rio Negro: Associação Kurikama Yanomami, 2019), http://bit.ly/3sFT50C (translation by the authors).

30 James Ferguson, *Global Shadows: Africa in the Neoliberal World Order* (Durham, NC: Duke University Press, 2006), 21.

31 "In Plain Sight," Diller Scofidio + Renfro, accessed March 2, 2021, https://dsrny.com/project/in-plain-sight.

32 See Noortje Marres, Michael Guggenheim, and Alex Wilkie, eds., *Inventing the Social* (Manchester: Mattering Press, 2018).

33 See Alan Weisman, *The World Without Us* (New York: Thomas Dunne Books/St. Martin's Press, 2007).

34 Stefanos Chen, "The Downside to Life in a Supertall Tower: Leaks, Creaks, Breaks," *New York Times*, February 3, 2021, https://www.nytimes.com/2021/02/03/realestate/luxury-high-rise-432-park.

35 See Boris Groys, *In the Flow* (London: Verso, 2016).

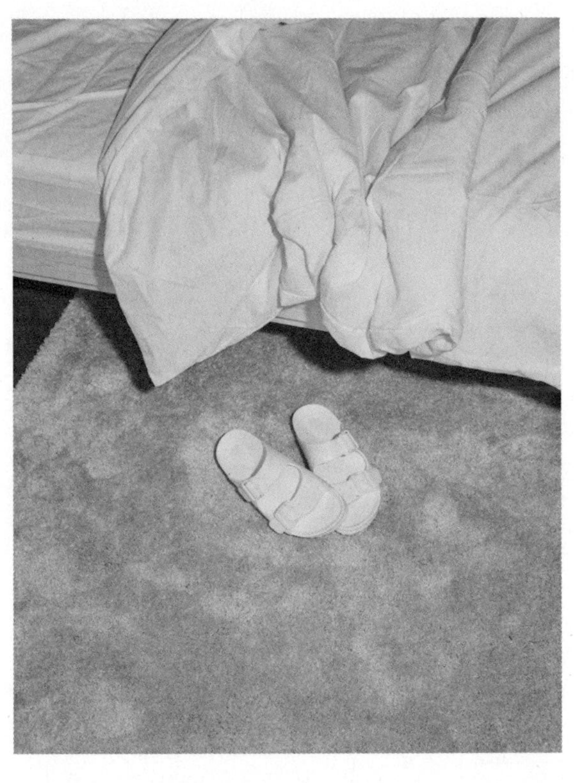

Everyday Life in the Diffuse House

Guillermo López and Anna Puigjaner (MAIO)

I'm staring at a Roomba; it has a tranquilizing effect. We have gotten used to these small gadgets sweeping our homes, the same way our ancestors in the first decade of the twentieth century got used to the strange vacuum cleaners taking the place of carpet sweepers in their households.[1] Since 2015, when iRobot introduced the Roomba 980, the first model connected to wireless internet, these little gizmos have been mapping out the limits and interiors of our homes and sending the information to company servers and onto third parties. Factors such as the size of the home, its location, the number of pieces of furniture, even the specific location of the children's room (usually the one with the most obstacles), when upscaled and transformed into big data, can start to render more things visible than we ever thought possible.

In a strange way, the information about our private realm has become public. Thanks to Roomba and its eerie data mapping, we can now imagine the possibility of creating a map of the interiors of the whole world.

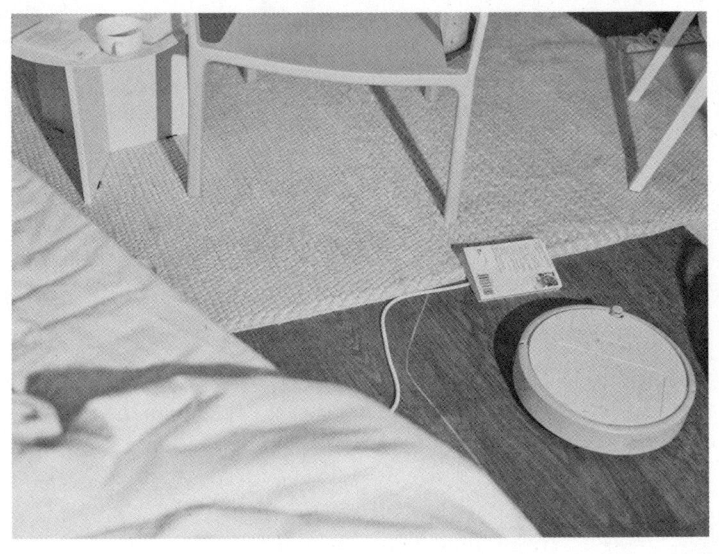

Just imagine an endless negative of Giambattista Nolli's eighteenth-century map of Rome, which detailed the floor plan of public buildings whereas the mass of domestic, "anonymous" architecture appeared as a muted poché. In reverse, in this potential new map generated by Roombas around the world, it is precisely the domestic space and its objects that are rendered visible.

Of course, this is just one example among many of how the image and nature of our domestic sphere have changed—especially if we still associate it with former notions of privacy and intimacy. The clear division between public and domestic spheres that appeared in Western territories during the Renaissance and experienced its heyday during the Enlightenment has become blurred. However, the line of demarcation between public and private has never been static; in fact, urban and domestic spheres have varied throughout history.[2]

In Roman law, the clear division between public and private echoed the dichotomy found in the Hellenistic world: the public sphere was solely incarnated by the polis and its politics, whereas the reproduction of life and everyday domestic labor, carried out by women and slaves, took place within the private sphere, which was strictly restricted to the house. The polis and the *oikos* (household) remained antithetical to the extent that any form of representation and visibility occurred exclusively within the public sphere of the polis.[3] This stark dichotomy vanished under the feudal lordships of the Middle Ages, when the distinction between public and private spheres was made nonexistent and, in regard to domestic space, many households were constituted by a single room that acted both as kitchen and bedroom, where all everyday life would occur.

Nevertheless, we can observe how the Renaissance, inspired by the Classical age, revised the relationship between public and private. From the sixteenth to the nineteenth century, the private sphere of the house grew increasingly antagonistic to the public sphere. It was with the emergence of the bourgeoisie and the modern state in Europe that the public sphere took on a new impulse and was redefined. In terms of space, the consolidation of the bourgeois public sphere—understood as a metaphorical place of assembly—did not always have a specific correlate: it emerged because of the appearance of public venues such as the first coffee houses and "domestic" private spaces such as the Parisian salons, where the intelligentsia would meet to discuss a new order of things. But despite this entanglement, from the sixteenth century on, what historians have defined as the "domestic system," a system in which the household remains the core of economic production, started to be considered preindustrial. This meant that labor and production were less and less connected to the domestic sphere. The separation of the workplace from the household became an almost universal feature of capitalist development.[4]

In this sense, if we compare our current late-capitalist situation with the emergence of the bourgeois public sphere and its clear demarcations, we may find ourselves in a moment in which both spheres, public and private, have not only converged, but where the assumptions relative to labor have invaded all corners of our households and lives. The process of this change can be traced back to the nineteenth century, during which the technification of the house, together with the implementation of modern functionalism, introduced scientific management logic to Western homes. Under this Fordist dream, mechanization and rationalization took command not only of kitchens but of domesticity at large. From Christine Frederick's pioneering experiments to the *Frankfurter Küche* and

Alexander Klein's diagrams, it is easy to witness how the standardization and quantification of everyday life became highly prescribed. The efficient logic of the factory came into the home. Every action was monitored, every distance measured, all our movements (especially women's) quantified and reduced as much as possible, always with the unfulfilled promise of reducing housework.

In terms of design, this was just the starting point for the forthcoming blueprints with which our homes were to be conceptualized. With the advent of late capitalism and a post-Fordist organization of society, every limit blurred following the new ideological and liberal motto of "flexibility." After the Second World War, the serialized, standardized, and repetitive methods proposed by Frederick Winslow Taylor and Frank and Lillian Gilbreth—increasingly rhetorical and Tati-esque—started to malfunction, which demanded a humanized redefinition in relation to everyday practices. However, the need for a renewed image of efficient capitalist methods was a necessary fiction that helped us cope with an increasingly generic and repetitive dehumanized environment, and this renewed image was, ultimately, a user-friendly interface that concealed similar (or even more sophisticated) principles of efficiency.

Certainly, this new idea of flexibility did not apply solely to the domestic realm. More and more flexible programs were implemented in different environments, including the field of corporate architecture. For instance, in 1958, the brothers Wolfgang and Eberhard Schnelle, assistants in their father's furniture company, decided to create their own company, the consulting and design firm Quickborner. Among the outstanding design concepts they produced, the idea of the *Bürolandschaft*, a new office layout (literally "office landscape"), stood out.[5] Thanks to mobile pieces of furniture and lightweight freestanding dividers, the organization of the space resulted in a relatively free distribution and zonification that went beyond the serialized rows of desks of the "American plan" model. It is true that the office landscape, although a completely new concept, did not alter many assumptions related to efficiency—for instance, hierarchies remained relatively untouched and closed offices were provided for executive managers. But in any case, the concept embodied the seamless transition from a Taylorist, factorylike environment to an easily transformable (potentially ever-changing) fantasy reminiscent of the domestic sphere.

The flexibility of the office space cannot be understood separately from the home, where the continuity of space started to be implemented as a consequence of the consolidation of post-Fordism in all actions and habits of everyday life. In the 1970s, many architectural attempts could be seen as an embodiment of the convergence of domestic and labor spheres. Think, for instance, of projects and exhibitions such as *Italy: The New Domestic Landscape* at New York's Museum of Modern Art in 1972, where the languages of the office and the household converged. A new home was presented in which coziness and spatial continuity went hand in hand with the logic of the workplace: inhabitable cubicles, modules, interior landscapes, expansive systems, and so on. Even the spatial continuity of the "zero ground level"—that is, the floor as an infinite plane—constituted a perfect endless horizontal display for the by-products of capitalism. Following the logic of the office and other consumerist typologies such as the mall, praise for continuity inundated the reflection on space.

Continuity became central to the new nonstop logic under which all spheres (public/private, labor/leisure, urban/domestic) converged.[6] This new diffuse scenario

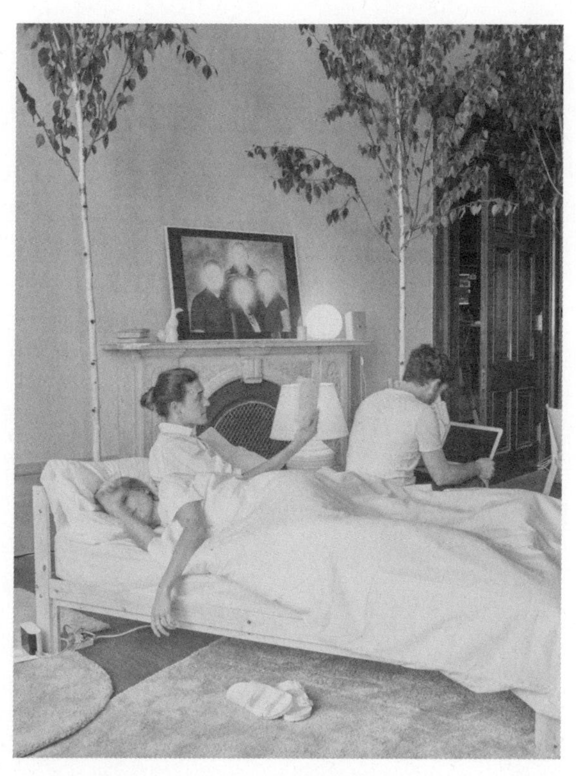

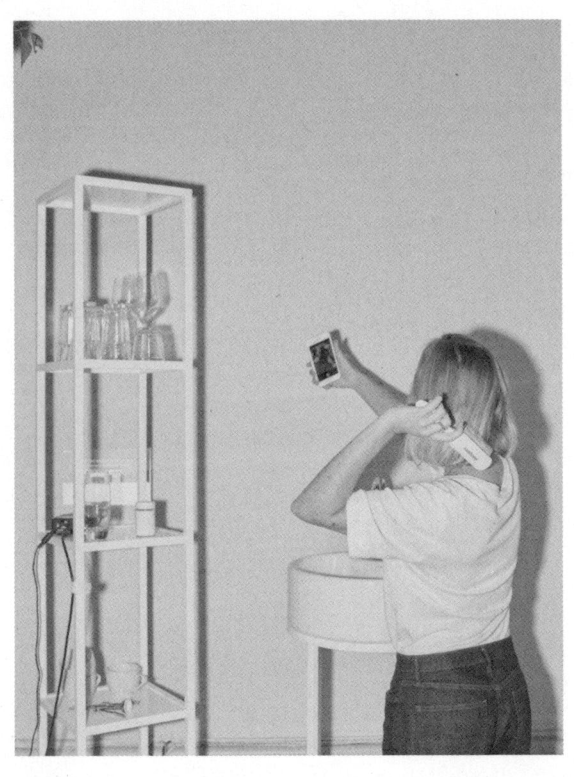

had an effect not only on our working and living spaces but also on our cities at large. While modernity based its ideas about urbanism and architecture on a precise set of hierarchical and prescribed forms of programmatic and spatial discontinuity, like the functional division of the modern city depicted in Le Corbusier's *The Athens Charter* (1933), under late capitalism the emerging forms of urbanism rely on an undifferentiated continuous model based on new economic formulas and systems of distribution.

If we take the *General Theory of Urbanization* (1867), written by Ildefons Cerdà, the engineer who planned Barcelona's urban grid, as one of the theoretical archetypes of the capitalist, potentially ever-growing modern city, we can witness the transformation of a society from artisanal to industrial. In the industrial city, the logic of decentralization and logistics was materialized by means of public facilities such as markets. These public and representative buildings were implemented in the city grid in two different scales—the scale of the neighborhood (every 25 blocks) and the scale of the district (every 100 blocks). These commons embodied the notion of the public sphere and public representation alongside (and contraposing) the "generic" buildings, which were mainly constituted by housing and tertiary services like offices.

Nowadays a similar transformation is occurring. Our society is changing from industrial to digital, and consequently the programs that used to be detached are merging in an atomized manner according to the logic of "last mile delivery": (precarious) gig economies lead to an (ad hoc) gig urbanism. The logic of this new logistics will shape our cities. We are moving toward an urbanism of shortened distances. In order for deliveries to be faster and more efficient, hubs and other small nodes have been progressively occupying leftover spaces, almost at a domestic scale—in many cases a by-product of the destructive and aggressive logic of "Amazonization." Paradoxically, Amazon and the like are becoming "local" (from Amazon Go to small distributing hubs), having destroyed the surplus of the now extinct shops and businesses.

These new atomized programs have filled the gaps in junkspace. Wastelands, *terrains vagues*, and vacant lots have been potentially phagocytosed by late capitalism and its technosphere. Never was junk so productive. Think, for instance, of the emergence of "dark kitchens"—kitchens closed to the public that cook food on demand, mainly for delivery companies—which have filled ground floors, basements, and even vacant parking lots. These formerly domestic elements now form a scattered urban system that has rendered visible the atomization and the blended form of urban domesticity. A system of cloud-connected elements producing (and even hiring) on demand in real time, like an eternal present.

Under this logic, the way we live has become more transient and fragile. It is not necessary to look back in time to realize that mobility has radically increased for both objects and citizens. Our objects are no longer stored inside cupboards, cellars, or closets, where it was relatively easy to access and use them. Instead, they have ended up filling Big Yellows, Bluespaces, and other self-storage units. They have become black-boxed and turned into invisible externalities, to the extent that they lose their potential use value. A profitable move when we consider how the rentability per square meter of storage spaces is in many cases higher than that of regular apartments, a fact that is pushing these storage units into city centers. In view of new tendencies practiced by companies such as Ikea, the status of all our objects might progressively change from property to rental. A form of digital feudalism that substitutes tithes for monthly subscriptions.

This diffuse urbanism cannot be detached from the immaterial labor and growing fragility of our liquefied relationships; it has become an environment in which labor and nonlabor converge at high speed. Speed is at home. Whereas in the 1980s Paul Virilio shaped the idea of dromocracy—that is, speed as a manifestation of power—today a subtle inversion has occurred when speed is applied to everyday life. We have experienced how velocity—think of couriers and deliveries—has become a sign of precarity. Only well-established classes can opt for slowness. The praise for slowness and other postmodern attempts to challenge late-capitalist velocity have not only been useless but have perpetuated existing forces of power and rendered visible their privileged status.

Amid this turmoil, the collective archetype that defines the image of our homes and the everyday life associated with it is rapidly changing. The postmodern dream of an isolated (and well-tempered) environment that promised architecture as an autonomous entity, and in turn urbanism as a set of discontinuous elements, has vanished. Think of a delirious New York presented as a compilation of wonderfully juxtaposed envelope buildings with astonishing free sections. Amid an unseen climate emergency, this fiction has faded before a more and more interconnected and fragile world. The domestic and the urban have merged in a diffuse and continuous reality. A new model forged by logistics has produced a much more atomized pattern where the entanglement of private and public has become deeper and deeper, moving toward something that requires our full attention and that might redefine the way we understand our future everyday life.

All images are part of the exhibition *Invisible Landscapes: Home (Act I)* at the Royal Academy of Arts, London, 2018. Photography by Ana Cuba. Courtesy of Royal Academy of Arts.

1 The detailed story of the relation of vacuum cleaners and other appliances to architecture can be read in Sigfried Giedion's seminal book *Mechanization Takes Command: A Contribution to Anonymous History* (Oxford: Oxford University Press, 1948).

2 See Jürgen Habermas, *The Structural Transformation of the Public Sphere: An Inquiry into a Category of Bourgeois Society*, trans. Thomas Burger with Frederick Lawrence (Cambridge: Polity Press, 1989).

3 See Hannah Arendt, *The Human Condition* (Chicago: University of Chicago Press, 1958), 28.

4 Michael McKeon, *The Secret History of Domesticity: Public, Private, and the Division of Knowledge* (Baltimore: Johns Hopkins University Press, 2007), 219.

5 See Nikil Saval, *Cubed: A Secret History of the Workplace* (New York: Doubleday, 2014).

6 See Jonathan Crary, *24/7: Late Capitalism and the Ends of Sleep* (London: Verso, 2013).

Wolff Architects, Cheré Botha School, Cape Town, 2017; roofed courtyard

Voids in the Everyday

Ilze and Heinrich Wolff
(Wolff Architects)

What are the core values that shape our practice and the work that emanates from it? As a married couple who has three children and who also works together, our daily lives have many overlaps. We wake up together, take the kids to school, and arrive at the office at the same time. In our daily routine, we are fortunate to be able to spend a lot of time together, both inside and outside the office. This is how it has been for many years. We are curious about other couples who work together when the work of each person is indistinguishable from the work of the other. That is not the case with us. Our minds find very different ways into the world of architecture, and our work methods and outputs are complimentary but never similar. Love and respect bind our collaboration much more than corresponding interests, approach, or output. Our life experiences have shaped the narratives of our work. The following stories have been written interchangeably by the two of us as a way to talk about our practice, Wolff Architects.

Being Aware of Selective Blindness

Our sense of everyday life, as South Africans, is not of a complete world. We do not experience the world as a

Heinrich Wolff, Langa, Cape Town, drawing from "Crime of Our Time" research project

perfectly formed honeycomb structure. For us, everyday life is like Swiss cheese, a matrix full of voids. These voids are not bubbles of nothingness; they are negations, denials, concealments, or disavowals of the everyday lives of others in the present or the past. These voids refer to worlds apart, or worlds removed; the social imagination of some that might be invisible to others. We are often blind to what is right in front of us.

A classic example is the selective blindness of the privileged. Architects often exacerbate situations of inequality by reproducing and enhancing orders of privilege without any real sense of the suffering they bring about. We recently produced a series of drawings to show how architects are complicit in escalating inequality in South Africa. In order to visualize this escalation, we developed a new method of drawing the city. Unlike Giambattista Nolli's eighteenth-century map of Rome, which shows all public spaces as universally accessible, and unlike the conventions surrounding architectural plans, which show all doors simultaneously open, this new method makes visible the restrictions placed on physical and economic mobility in South African cities. It develops the hypothesis put forth by theorist Irit Rogoff and the freethought collective that infrastructures govern "just as much and perhaps more than political ideologies and rhetoric." These drawings aim to expose how infrastructures can prevent as much as enable. Spaces of disconnection, devoid of opportunity, are shown in black. Open, public space under democratic control is drawn in white. Each privately owned property is shown in a different color to show the scale and multitude of ownerships. This study proposes that the creation of economic opportunity is as important an urban infrastructure as engineering.

There are other kinds of voids in the everyday; voids where things were removed from the world.

A South African example is forced removals: people were racially classified and segregated, and subsequently neighborhoods were demolished or public buildings such as theaters and cinemas were closed. The forced removals leave a real void in the city and real pain in the hearts of the victims. As time moves on, this void is unfortunately not equally visible to everyone.

For me, the most urgent aspect of our research is to document that which has been lost. The residual material world alludes to another world yet at the same time is an explicit disavowal of that world: a Black world, a female world, a queer world, and a communal world. As a Black female student at the University of Cape Town, I recognized this disavowal early on in my architectural training. I have since developed ways to advocate for both the return of and to that world, and at the same time imagine contemporary versions thereof. The publication format is one way in which we, as Wolff Architects, begin this reinsertion with our collaborators. I started *pumflet: art, architecture and stuff* because we could see very little public atonement and recognition of the spatial injustices of the past by the patrons of architecture or architects themselves. The publications that circulate among us in the profession focus on congratulating technical achievements of built and urban form or serve as self-proclaimed "neutral" repositories of contemporary architectural production but are then inevitably dominated by projects of our privileged white male colleagues. I purposefully distanced our practice from this false neutrality and created a publication that would be intentionally personal yet pay homage to the communal. The format is analogue but it would be freely available within all spheres, including the digital. It would seek to publish loss while equally recognizing the achievements made despite such loss. Our publications are thus a collection of my personal obsessions that provoke

Cover of *pumflet: art, architecture and stuff*, "Gladiolus," 2016–17

collective thinking: a demolished movie house down the road from our office (the installment "Alabama"); a seaside settlement built by Black descendants of the enslaved and West African migrant dockworkers in the early twentieth century that was destroyed during apartheid's grand plan of forced and racialized urban relocations ("Gladiolus"); a writer's house and garden in Serowe, Botswana, that tells the story of creation amid violent isolation, expulsion, and destruction ("Summer Flowers").[2] Through *pumflet*, together with others I work through and meditate on these spatial narratives as a way for the architectural practice to gain wisdom and an ethical stance on how to intervene consciously and sensitively in a place like South Africa. As architects, it is our imperative to remain conscious of the interventions of the past (and the present) in order to produce spaces that engender life, pay homage to lost communal practices, and inevitably participate in the important work of repair.

Our practice is trying to make visible what has been concealed, to reveal what has been covered, and to build connections where there are voids.

The Economy of Cities

When I was a boy, I would cycle across a field to my grandparents' house. I loved this open space because it had dirt mounds that we could ride over with our bikes. Until a mall was built. I lost my playground, which upset me, and over time I grew even more disenchanted—the mall sucked all the successful businesses out of our city. The mall thrived and the city suffered. The mall became the place for the affluent, the city the place of the poor. The city I enjoyed as a child was wrecked. My shock at the planned destruction of the city led me to my thesis topic: "The Destruction of the Typology of the Shopping Mall."

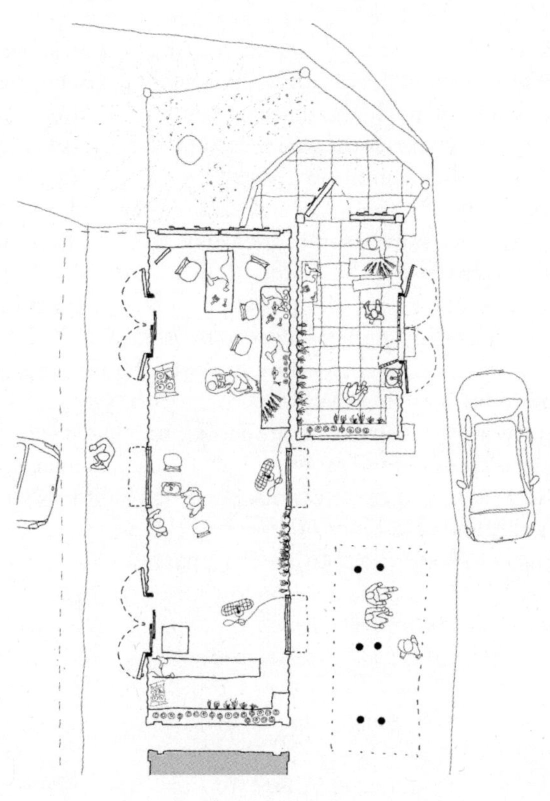

Heinrich Wolff, Zama's Hair Salon, drawing from
"Ways of Living" research project, 2016

Jane Jacobs's *The Economy of Cities* (1969) inspired me to think about what kind of city supports the kind of economy we would like to have.

Years later, while working on a school in Du Noon, Cape Town, I saw very small-scale apartments (6–12 m^2 each), where the rentals were equivalent (per square meter) to the highest rentals in upmarket areas of the city. This led to a decade-long study of the correlation between economic activity and the spaces that support it in an impoverished Cape Town neighborhood. I studied the spaces and economies of shops, bars, streets, churches, mosques, day-care centers, and public transport hubs. Among many other things, this study taught me the power of small-scale trading spaces in providing easy access to the urban economy.

At the time of the study, we were appointed to design a business incubator in Cape Town. We were excited by the possibility that such an incubator, which claims to advance and grow businesses, can produce the urban corollary of these claims. We proposed that it lift its activities off the ground, clearing the way for a large market of small-scale businesses. Instead of making a building, we expanded the urban network. Instead of giving the building a distinct appearance, we tried to create infrastructure for economic activity.

Social Superstructure

Most of the public buildings we have been involved in over the years are designed to be adaptable over time. They invite user participation and mutation rather than attempt to be masterpieces for future conservation. The spaces are densely populated and used intensely. The budget never seems to be large enough to make everything nice in the building, and one has to be strategic about where to spend money and where to save it. This has led us to a strategy

Wolff Architects, Watershed market, Cape Town, 2014; interior view

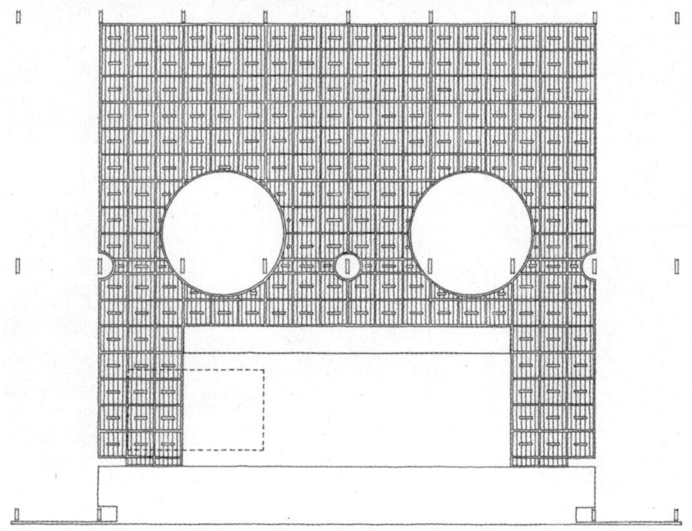

Wolff Architects, Watershed market, Cape Town, 2014; inverted ceiling plan

of designing superstructures and substructures. The superstructure is the durable infrastructure that defines the architecture and allows for the substructure to be adaptable and low-cost. The superstructure must be more than just a structure and service highways; it must define the order of the architecture and facilitate the primary social and urban gestures of the building. In densely occupied spaces we've found that the floors and walls are often hardly visible or dematerialized by intense use. In other words: people dominated rather than architectural form. We therefore elect to use the ceiling as the principal social superstructure. It is a surface that is not changed often and can be shaped to facilitate the kind of social life required by the institution and the city. The ceiling is also a surface that can create the right kind of light to activate the desired social life of the space below. The roofs covering the ceilings of the superstructure are often quite simple.

For us, paying attention to the stories of our society, both personal and collective, becomes a way to gather the wisdom of how to intervene in ethical ways in spaces where we still feel the residues of trauma. As a practice, we demand of ourselves to be fully informed and pay attention to the details and nuances of these residues. Although we cannot claim to have gathered all the wisdom required to intervene successfully each time, in this essay we have shared some of the ways we relate our craft to the world. Our approach is to recognize the voids as residues of extreme misanthropic actions and then go about our everyday practice of architecture by working on the project of repair and restorative spatial justice. Our work finds its ways in advocacy (engaged architectural publications and public culture) as well as in the manner in which we implement the designs of buildings (superstructures and reprogramming the economies of cities).

Anna Heringer and Eike Roswag-Klinge, METI school, Rudrapur, Bangladesh, 2007; view of the caves, 2019

Resourceful Architecture

Anna Heringer

As an architect, I believe that design is a tool to impact lives. In that sense, I consider myself a humanist activist as well, inasmuch as I believe in human nature beyond ethnicities. Every natural creation deals with three aspects: energy, materiality, and information. I understand alternative energy as being not solely solar or green, but also human. Labor is, for me, a vital part of design. For this reason, my projects enable many people to participate and share a building's budget. I look for materials that emerge from a place as indigenous resources. Local information, the seat of know-how, is also an aspect that my work focuses on. Yet I believe that knowledge and creativity should not be limited to a certain place but instead should be shared as a global resource. Reapplying this global "asset" to other local resources and circumstances is the strategy I have been trying to implement through design.

I inherited this trinity—energy, materiality, and information—from my father, an ecologist and landscape designer who values things that already exist in nature. However, when I began my professional life, I needed to find evidence for these convictions. I ended up unearthing evidence in Bangladesh, which represented a milestone in my career trajectory. While carrying out volunteer work there, in particular with Dipshikha, a nongovernmental organization for rural development, I learned how to make the best out of existing resources rather than relying on external systems. For my thesis project seven years later, I designed a school out of earth and bamboo for Dipshikha. The METI (Modern Education and Training Institute) school, realized from 2005 to 2006 with Eike Roswag-Klinge and craftsmen from Rudrapur, is based on a concept that instills self-confidence and independence in children with the aim of strengthening their sense of identity. Where life is focused on the essentials, circular energy, materiality, and information have a more direct impact on both society and the individual. Taken out of my usual context of Bavaria, I was able to see things with not only curious but also sharper eyes. This displacement allowed me to find beauty and wisdom beyond the ordinary, something one tends to overlook in one's own context.

Love versus Fear, Life versus Death

After my experience in Bangladesh, I was able to reorient my work through the matrix of energy, materiality, and information without needing to rely on a green-building certification program or fair-trade label. I have been assessing my own level of sustainability, translating design into a joint effort with others. In the end, it all comes down to a harmonious coexistence with nature and other human beings. It is incredible how fear-driven German design is on issues related to maintenance and durability: when it comes to participation, liability is all that matters. Every decision that is based on fear—the fear of being sued, for example—is definitely a bad decision. At the same time, decay should not be undermined. We have to be in tune with life, which also includes death: we should always design the decay of a building. The core of the

Anna Heringer and Martin Rauch, Cathedral of Worms rammed earth altar, Germany, 2018

sustainability debate is to overcome our own personal fears. I consider sustainability to be not a technical or economic issue but an issue related to affection and care. Hence, decisions should be made out of love—love for the other and for the environment—rather than out of fear.

When it comes to the relation between costs and people's needs in view of questions of sustainability, resource assessment, and distribution, it is important to acknowledge the existence of materials that are globally available at very low or no cost. Mud, for instance, is everywhere. The energy it requires is human labor—which is available in abundance. Earth can be deployed in construction using high-tech or low-tech modes without carbon dioxide or electricity or with large, sophisticated 3-D printers. These factors can be combined, making mud applicable in any context. In fact, there is no real argument against building with mud. What is missing is information. It is crucial to define what is contemporary earthen architecture, a term that refers to one of the oldest traditional technologies employing earthen materials. If 10 percent of the material mix is cement and the rest is mud, considering that normal concrete consists of 12 percent cement, can it still be called earthen architecture or mud architecture? There needs to be a more critical conversation about these definitions.

I have developed a design method in collaboration with Martin Rauch, clay storming, which entails a more intuitive approach to matter: design based on material understanding. This is a process that has the potential to change architectural criteria regarding precision and detail. It consists of manually working on large clay models to stimulate our perception and allow our creativity to flow. I have been trying to gear my work toward the dissemination of knowledge that is associated with these earthen technologies. With a few trained workers on-site, it is easy to teach unskilled laborers practically rather than theoretically. However, it is difficult to bring these technologies into the curriculum of Western architecture and engineering schools, which are still based on theory rather than on-site experience. And while these technologies are still the reality for many—many rely on mud to provide shelter—the know-how might be lost if it misses a generation because of a series of circumstances, including the lobbying of cement and steel companies.

Yet I consider it possible to scale up these earthen building technologies. This is why it matters that, in all sorts of countries and societies, public buildings should be designed with bamboo, mud, or timber to change the image of these traditional everyday materials. For me, mud is more than just a material or technology, it is also a response to social justice and climate change. The same way a project such as the METI school in Bangladesh is much more than a building: it is a collective enterprise that is capable of creating jobs and redistributing construction costs to day laborers and craftspeople who can, in turn, reinvest them in the local market. The capital that is deployed for construction sites of buildings employing local materials can act as a real catalyst for homegrown markets and small economies.

Local Affections and Global Networks

I have been building my own arguments based on these collective building experiences, with both reason and emotions. People want to live in a beautiful and comfortable home, whether it is designed in brick or concrete, for emotional reasons rather than technological concerns. I take these needs and dreams very seriously. Coming from the international-aid scene, I am wary of imposing models that are driven

Anna Heringer and Eike Roswag-Klinge, METI school, Rudrapur, Bangladesh, 2007; external view of the facade, 2019

through institutions and the media, as has been the case throughout centuries of colonialism and so-called missionary work. To counter this logic, I understood that the affective experience of building and inhabiting space is the most convincing argument. Yet, although my work aims to produce these experiences with local resources and solutions, it does have a global perspective that attempts to connect these emotional and subjective networks.

On-site, I start with the local materials, local know-how, and local energy resources. I see myself as a vessel for expertise, because I am not inventing; rather, I am preserving and combining things in a different way, not only across the globe, but also across time. *Mudworks*, the exhibition I cocurated in 2012 with Martin Rauch, reenforced the potential of rammed earth by presenting it as high-tech and based on a natural resource, with capacities and limits like any other technology or material. It acts differently in each context—Bangladeshi mud is different from Austrian mud. Creative forms and solutions come out of the variety of local parameters intrinsically related not only to climate but also to the tools available. Embracing limits, constraints, and vulnerability is a meaningful principle, similar to finding the right tools—not to change the material, not to stabilize it or make it less mutable, but to adjust the language of design. It is crucial to adjust mud technology to the specifics of the context in which one operates; it lends itself to this because of its resilience.

Contemporary Archaisms

I consider mud technology to be an archaism that is contemporary rather than associated with the brutalist idiom of raw materials such as concrete. Today everything is built so fast, so randomly, fully disconnected to the realities of our time—not even out of context, but without context. I thus long for this archaic feeling of authenticity. It is something that plays a strong role in my work, along with a consideration for Maslow's hierarchy of needs, since participation is one of the many levels of human needs. Every child builds a hut, a tent, their own nest and shelter—this is what it means to be human, it is engraved in our DNA. A playhouse that is store-bought or made by parents for their children is never as interesting as what the children can build themselves. As architects, we have to provide space for this ludic notion and need to once again allow people to take part in the construction of their own home. This is in line with the use of resources. Mud, bamboo, and timber are materials that allow for collective engagement. These archaic needs, forms, patterns, and materials are core components of what I design. At the same time, ornaments and playful elements are important to make things desirable. Once I participated in making an elaborated rammed-earth structure and next to it a playhouse for the neighborhood kids. Children came and decorated the structure with marbles and small mirrors in a playful way. It was liberating to not have to control everything. It is a beautiful operation that happens *in loco*: not to design something so that someone else can build it, but instead to be on-site with people who take part in the whole process.

When I designed the METI school in Bangladesh, I first imagined that I could draw inspiration from the aforementioned archaic shapes that play into children's imagination: nests, treehouses, caves. In the second design stage, I realized that it is equally important for the children to take part in the entire building process. Although their participation did result in quite a bit of chaos, the creative process entailed in the making of their own school out of dirt with their own hands

Women participating in the construction of the Anandaloy Building, 2019

provided them with feelings of ownership, pride, and confidence that would not have come about otherwise. This was a rather normal procedure for different societies in the past, and it still is for some in the present: a community coming together to build its own school, church, mosque, or temple. Those moments, which triggered a common dignity and unity, could also provide for the care of their built environment. Architecture has a huge impact on that—nothing is more empowering than standing in front of a beautiful building that you helped build with your own hands. I think as a society we lack those incredibly powerful occasions and experiences. Indeed, many aspects of my design come from these moments of collaboration and a slower-paced way of intervening in the planet.

Resourceful Participation

I was once asked how this approach, advocating purportedly archaic methods and slow-paced performances, could respond to today's housing crisis. I recalled my visit to a Rohingya refugee camp in Bangladesh, where the need for housing is extreme. I was struck by the fact that the camp was waiting for materials to be shipped from abroad while people were literally sitting on building resources. To bring in know-how that would enable people to build their own house at a slightly slower pace would mean not only responding to an urgent need but also providing a healing process. Housing is more than just four walls and a roof: it is a right. Exercising this right could become an empowering and holistic procedure for community building, a procedure that could help deal with the vulnerabilities, traumas, and wounds caused by genocide.

This is not just a matter of speed, of how fast one can react. Participation in architecture, for me, is

Anna Heringer and Eike Roswag-Klinge, METI school, Rudrapur, Bangladesh, 2007; external view of the stairs, 2019

linked with the idea of a hierarchy of the intellect over the hand. There is a lot of nonverbal communication on-site, which can be very productive, because words are often problematic, particularly when not all of those involved speak the same language. This is similar to how participation in a democracy is not just about voting or protesting—it is also about making constructive actions together.

For the discipline of architecture, in turn, these premises and methods also have the potential to change the daily practice of architects, from the scope of design to hierarchies and detailing. Perfection is a killer for participation as well as for trust. When a design concept is strong and harmonious, imperfection can even be an asset. Beauty and imperfection are qualities that resonate with people.

I believe in a global strategy for sustainability. Not a high-tech approach that is only affordable for a small part of the world's population. We live on one planet, we are one humankind. Why should we work and build differently, using more material resources in Germany than in Bangladesh, for example, just because we can afford it financially? We as human beings are responsible for these resources: how we extract them and creatively employ them for their own subsistence, and therefore our own subsistence. This of course calls for change, and change is always uncomfortable, especially if you are on the sunny side of the conjuncture. If someone were to ask me, "If, as an architect, you have at your disposal a hundred million to make a difference in the world, what would you do?" I would answer that architects actually do have the financial resources at their disposal. Not in one bundle but throughout their career, if they add up all the building budgets they've been responsible for. They just need to be aware of that, and make the right decisions in every project. I strongly believe that the world changes not with one big decision but with everyday gestures and decisions made out of respect for human beings, for the planet and its ecosystems, and, just as importantly, made out of trust rather than fear.

This essay is a transcription of an interview conducted by Vanessa Grossman, Charlotte Malterre-Barthes, and Ciro Miguel; it was edited by Vanessa Grossman.

An aerial view of Mouraria 53 (in the center) surrounded by neighboring buildings, including a bar that hosts drag shows, a tenement house, and a series of medical-equipment stores, Salvador, Brazil, 2018

Networking Resources

Mouraria 53

In December 2016, when we first entered Mouraria 53, it was a forest within a structure. We would soon convince its owners, who had already accepted the acquisition of the house as a hopeless mistake, to agree to an unlikely exchange: for four years they would lend their ruin to our collective—young people inexperienced in construction—and expect in return a functional house.[1] Out of this agreement, an experiment was born. We named our collective after the address of the experiment—its only coherent feature. The members and purpose of Mouraria 53 have changed over the years—we are designers, psychologists, cultural producers, photographers, architects, sociologists, lawyers, and musicians. Architecture, as we see it, can be the sum of these activities.

Networks of people, knowledge, and materials interact to make a construction. In a sense, they are the construction itself: to understand them is to assemble the collisions in which the possibility of making things arises. This obsessive tracing of architecture in its essentially nonarchitectural encounters—the methodology of our practice—follows recent developments in sociology and a new way of understanding disciplines that were previously isolated. Bruno Latour's article in *Le Monde* in March 2020, for example, while commenting on the nature of the COVID-19 catastrophe, argued against the notion of a deadly virus.[2] For him, the rates of both transmission and mortality reflected a network in which property rights for scientific developments, the availability of hospital beds and masks, tourism, and urban densities were as important as molecules and atoms. Our architecture becomes possible in the hopelessness of property owners—and in our own hopelessness as recent graduates without job possibilities in the midst of an economic meltdown. Architectures of crisis must seek new resources. Ours is everyday life.

Mouraria 53 is currently a psychology clinic, art gallery, scenography storage, and yoga school; up until recently it was also an artist residency.[3] Events happen on a weekly basis (workshops, concerts, music-video and photo shoots). On weekends, a collective of photographers works on building a darkroom for developing film. The artist residency was set up in 2019, and for six months a group of women recorded the sounds of construction in the house (later turning the recordings into electronic music).[4] In the front of the building, a woman and her son sell lottery tickets. A fruit seller used to store his goods in our garage.[5] Iago, the psychologist, works with homeless people, holding monthly meetings in the house. A jazz band, a rap group, and two university professors are also among the regular collaborators.[6] Mouraria 53 has an Instagram page, a logo, a shared Google Drive, and some fifteen overlapping WhatsApp groups. Finally, there is Salvador, a city whose contributions are too many to count.

The sum of those may be an architecture, or a need for it to exist. The opposite is also true: architecture allows for relationships to take place (quite literally). We've learned to tell its stories. If there is any relevance to Mouraria 53, it is that of a practice that, like Latour's (as a sociologist, philosopher, anthropologist, and artistic creator), consciously engages with the broader field in order to act. This approach—valid as long as it is not done by architects single-handedly—may be useful in dealing with resources and their crisis, especially since the networks through which masks, beds, food, or windows enter our lives have become completely abstract.

Desire and Encounter

To generate hope within the hopeless, we inhabit. Our experiment is, among other things, a social one. The program of Mouraria 53 was not predefined, rather it was a result of its interactions: people come to the ruin bringing their dreams, construction takes place through exchange—or simply for fun, as with the lawyers who helped with wrecking walls—and in the meantime encounters happen. Progressively, as experiences become linked, the physical ruin becomes a subjective palace.

Encounters lead to collaboration: photographers who met during construction set up a collective; a band and an artist made an album cover together; concertgoers sign up for therapy sessions; yoga teachers bring construction materials to the house. Some exchanges drive construction: music groups work on the house so they can use it as a venue; artists make useful site-specific installations as part of their exhibitions; professors bring students to work and gain practical knowledge. Inhabiting the house gives its existence purpose—it progressively becomes an exquisite corpse of the dreams produced within it. In this process, architecture must cope with the unpredictable. It should also become a tool of faith, since motivation for building will depend on believing the task to be possible.

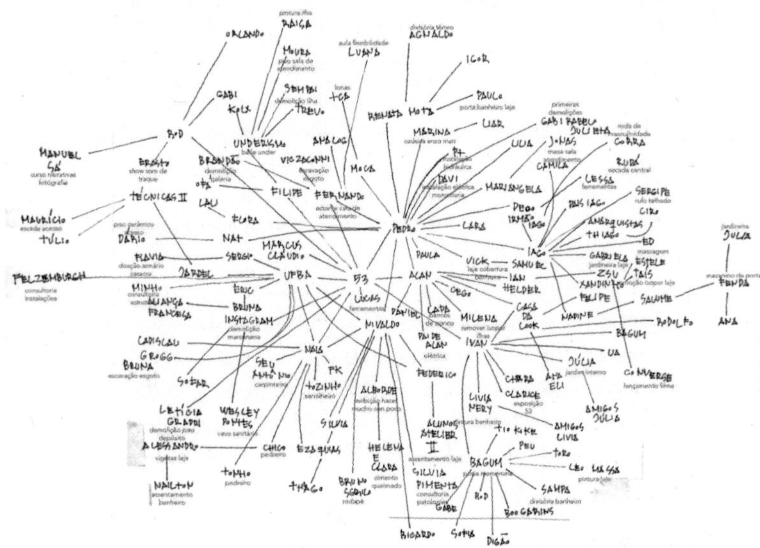

Mouraria 53, diagram of people, materials, and construction "authorship," 2018

The Great Wall of China was built in a series of stretches of a few kilometers in order to nurture accomplishments within a task bigger than the life of its workers; similarly, we build the house not in layers (structure, finishings, electrical installation) but in a series of acts to be inhabited immediately. Living as we build produces hope within our unlikely economic reality (for both the owners and the team), and it also acknowledges the possibility that plans can change. The strategy is somewhat inspired by Brazilian self-construction: favela houses with *lajes* incorporate a sense of possibility into the "final" architecture—if a son or daughter is born, construction may start on top of the house—entangling genealogy, desire, and construction.[7] For us, however, building in acts is not an unplanned emergency but a process of compulsive design. A member of the collective breaks up with his girlfriend, turning an office into a temporary bedroom; as his life reassembles and he moves out, the previous home is turned into a tattoo studio. All stages of the process are designed and dreamed.

Designing for chance becomes a daily or weekly practice; like (and learning from) therapy and photo-journalism, it also allows for improvisation (like rap and jazz) and a dissolution of authorship. We believe some of it to be expandable toward less experimental practices. Architects as providers of a service—instead of a product—are essential for architecture in our age.

Our ensemble, it must be mentioned, is not always romantic. It is chaotic when lots of people do different things: noise from the installation of exhibitions bothers the psychologists, and dust from the construction annoys the residents (the structure of these feuds is often a clash between the house as an event and the house as a perennial habitat). Encounters are simultaneously our crisis and resource.

We are based in Salvador, a metropolis in northeastern Brazil. As in most Brazilian cities, formal and informal construction radically superimpose different ways of living that share common material dreams. Concrete, bricks, and large ceramic tiles have, over the decades, acquired the connotation of security and wealth. As a result, the city is engulfed in a spiral of obsolescence—for instance, wooden floors and windows from modernist gems become garbage. Our engagement with reuse was pragmatic—we had no money—yet it gradually became conceptual. Our Instagram campaign "What You Don't Want May Be Useful to Us" revealed that, in a city that does not recycle, building cheap meant using noble materials from various demolition sites. Building the house from the city made the latter an index of the former—in terms of its culture (the materials that were becoming unfashionable or unusable), its economy, and its memories.

The city, according to the discourse of reuse, is a quarry—yet this metaphor is imprecise. Though a part of Brazilian obsolescence is deeply embedded in the architectural dreams of its citizens, it is also a result of the more general conflict between the time frames of the contemporary labor-divided (between those who design and those who build) construction industry and the erratic nature of urban storage—one never knows which materials will become available. In their book *Déconstruction et réemploi* (2017), Rotor, a Belgium-based office engaged in reuse activism in Europe, addresses this problem from the perspective of research (investigating cycles of obsolescence to predict what will be disposed), building information modeling, and public policy. Their practice, however, disregards analogous changes that could take place in architectural practices—namely, the incorporation of chance.

If designing for a changing public means routinely drawing different possibilities, designing while considering changes in resources demands drawing to convey ideas instead of teleological renderings. Tags in a floor plan may indicate doubt—for instance, "This could be a window."[8] Designing with what is given is also achieved through paranoia: "Everything we have becomes everything we need." Door becomes floor, floor becomes window, window becomes wall, and wall becomes floor. If contemporary architecture is often understood as a language of elements—the architect being an assembler of a catalogue—our process deals with the connotations of its use.

For us, materials are also resources of what they bring from their previous lives—Hello Kitty stickers on the inside of a window, traces of impact on the stage floor of Brazil's first modernist theater, even a story told by a donor. In our architecture, as well in exhibitions and pedagogical experiments, these stories became valuable. Our recognition of this has been influenced by the work of artists and a genealogy of architects from Salvador that conducted simultaneous practices in scenography and formal construction (a superimposition that made the ephemeral a test for the permanent and the permanent the residue of an event).[9]

Wooden floors and windows are also evidence of vanishing techniques—by-products of the cultural obsolescence that we encounter in our attempts to reuse them. As industrialization and cheap aggregated materials take over (continuous with a larger failure at all levels of the Brazilian education system, including the technical), knowledge is lost.

Networks of Knowledge

Despite being an archive of physical materials, Mouraria 53 is possible only in a world of digital practices. Social

Members of Mouraria 53 demolishing a wall to set up a stage for their concert, 2018

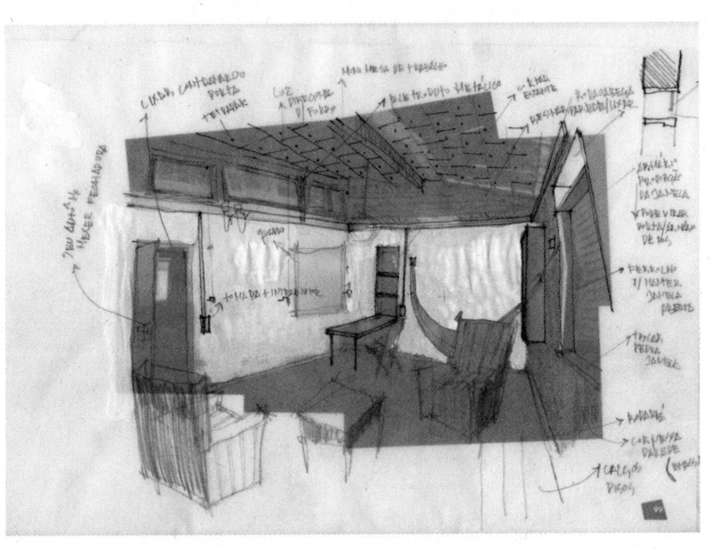

Mouraria 53, sketch for the psychology clinic inside the collective, designed with minimal resources, 2018

media enables collective construction to be managed and materials to be gathered; it also accounts for our connection with different collectives in Brazil as well as Latin America. YouTube especially has set a new paradigm for the universe of self-construction. The range of tutorials on the video platform is enormous and nationally defined: retired European and Australian gentlemen assemble Leroy-Merlin ready-mades; Brazilian *pedreiros* or construction workers teach brick and concrete favela construction, including advice to those wondering "whether or not to build above my parents"; suburban Americans display their "hobbies" in sheds with what, for people in other countries, would be heavy-industry machinery. In Brazil, the shift from what used to be a system of apprenticeship is surely emancipatory—our experiment and the inclusion of women in construction, for instance, have become possible[10]—but also dangerous, as general instructions might be followed uncritically.

Knowledge is both a resource and a network. We hire traditional craftspeople as teachers (our budget is almost entirely spent on transportation of materials and workforce knowledge). Their way of making things influences ours—it shapes the detail of present and future designs. University professors incorporate these craftspeople into their pedagogical process by bringing their students to build with them. The university faculty also acts as a consultancy, compensating our poor knowledge in construction. Craftsmen and professors frequently contradict each other. Antônio, our carpenter, was responsible for our reassembly of the house's original staircase in a different room, an operation considered impossible by academics.

Finally, the digital condition allows an Ecuadorian architect's Instagram stories to become, within weeks, a construction experiment in Salvador-Bahia. The staircase for our darkroom (used by Analog, the

Initially used as an office, the editing station incorporated a leftover space between the slab and floor for a capsule bed at Mouraria 53, 2018

Mouraria 53, stairway collectively assembled from parts of different staircases, 2019

photography collective, to process film) is an open-source element designed by Al Borde—whose 2014 House in Construction project inspired and informed our experiment. Extensive knowledge means architects can refuse some requirements for constant originality.

A House

Mouraria 53 is a hundred years old. It was built at the beginning of the twentieth century in an area surrounding Salvador's historic settlement from 1550 (the first settlement in Brazil). In 1937, upon the death of its owner, who was Catholic, it was donated to the church. After years of neglect, it was auctioned off. Fourteen years later, we came in.

As we stripped the walls of the ruin, memories of the city resurfaced: different kinds of bricks from an industrial past lay alongside adobe blocks and tram tracks from the old public transit system, salvaged and used as lintels; family initials and drawings were hidden under layers of paint. The donation of the house by the former owner tells a story of religious presence—the church still holds more than two hundred properties in Salvador's center—and its devaluation tells of the urban sprawl of the 1970s.[11] Its patchwork construction reveals a different time in architecture, before the madness of concrete emerged as a standard of quality. Looking back after four years, our process has more to do with the memory of Mouraria 53 than with the productions of contemporary real estate. It also presents a critique of current models of environmentalism. The "sustainable architecture" checklist relies on the false premise of life-cycle assessments—a methodology in which the environmental costs of buildings are estimated in hundred-year life spans. High-cost low-maintenance elements (such as concrete) become "sustainable" only if the many other reasons for sub-

Filipe Duarte and Raísa Muniz, a couple who joined Mouraria 53 in 2018, are currently building a house with materials and designs supplied by the relationships established through the collective, 2020

tracting or changing buildings are ignored. Mouraria 53, before and after our intervention, tells a story in which fashion, politics, real estate, and a disappearing workforce (i.e., the impossible maintenance of parquet floors in Salvador) are more common than natural material decay.

All attempts to explain what we do result in a false anatomy. There's no real separation between materials, people, and knowledge: we learn by understanding how a window was assembled, we live next to Antônio, our carpenter, and the materials we use are defined by what we know and are. Our photography, more journalistic than architectural, is often more telling—yet it is no substitute for being in the house.

1 Our initiative was inspired by a similar project, House in Construction (2014), by the Ecuadorian architectural practice Al Borde. The owners contributed 10,000 US dollars to our experiment—about a tenth of the amount necessary if the project were done by formal means.

2 Bruno Latour, "La crise sanitaire incite à se préparer à la mutation climatique," *Le Monde*, March 25, 2020, https://www.lemonde.fr/idees/article/2020/03/25/la-crise-sanitaire-incite-a-se-preparer-a-la-mutation-climatique_6034312_3232.html.

3 Mouraria 53 is presently composed of Alan dos Anjos, Dário Sales, Fernando Gomes, Filipe Duarte, Iago Lobo, Pedro Alban, and Rodrigo Sena, who all coauthored this text. Previous members of the collective are Davi Fernandes, Ivan Depasiri, Jonas Ximenes, Júlia Bittencourt, Milena Abreu, and Pedro Teixeira.

4 The tracks can be heard on the group's SoundCloud page, https://soundcloud.com/user-467645504.
5 In exchange, we used his van to pick up donated materials. The arrangement was interrupted because of a fruit-related rat problem.
6 Bagum's and Underismo's music can be heard on Spotify. Bagum filmed a video in the house; see "BAGUM live at Mouraria53," YouTube video, February 21, 2019, 19:52, https://www.youtube.com/watch?v=WrhSDbEpWX4&ab_channel=BAGUM.
7 *Lajes* are structural slabs on top of informal housing. Because of their panoramic views, they are often featured in funk and rap music videos—a recurring image that for many has come to symbolize the favela.
8 Our drawings' tags are also pedagogical inserts, replacing the irregular knowledge in reading plans with our common experience of living in the house (i.e., "the red square is where we took our picture").
9 These architects include Sete43, Renata Mota, Marcos Nunez, and Cinthia Rosa.
10 Paloma Cipriano has a YouTube channel with over a million followers where she teaches standard construction techniques such as bricklaying. See, for instance, Paloma Cipriano, "COMO REBOCAR PAREDE – How to tow wall – DIY – Paloma Cipriano," YouTube video, September 26, 2016, 6:50, https://www.youtube.com/watch?v=11pwVuMpCp0&t=12s. The inclusion of women in construction will have an impact on the material dimensions of the

industry—the currently standard fifty-kilogram cement bag needs to be carried by a body that will no longer be the norm; for our collective, carrying it was impossible. The investigation of architecture and its building bodies is characteristic of the system of prefabricated school buildings that João Filgueiras Lima, a.k.a. Lelé, developed for Salvador.

11 From the 1970s on, the city of Salvador abandoned its historic center, moving its commercial and administrative activities to other parts of the city. Lina Bo Bardi's projects in Salvador during the 1980s were part of a larger (but unsuccessful) attempt to revert the situation. In the 1990s, Salvador's historic center once again became the focus of administrative attention—this time through a problematic tourist-based approach.

Zak Group, spatial/political layout of the House of Lords, Upper House of the Parliament of the United Kingdom, Palace of Westminster, London, 2015

Crossbenching and Publics (and Their Assemblies)

Markus Miessen (Studio Miessen)

> The crossbench politician tries, in fact, to avoid taking sides by following a clearly individualistic position. I always insist that to act politically is to act as part of an "us," to act from the position of a "we." Your position in that sense could be compared to someone intervening from the outside—a role that is similar to somebody who wants to mediate a conflict.
>
> —Chantal Mouffe[1]

The last twenty years have seen a huge increase in the methods and protocols with which architects and urbanists have attempted to participate in (geo)political spatial conditions that were not previously considered part of their job description. Simultaneously, interest in architecture and urbanism has increased massively in a plethora of fields that used to be clearly delineated—geography, sociology, political philosophy, urban policy, artistic and curatorial practices—which suggests a movement toward a refined understanding of the importance and difficulties of engaging directly in the production of space—in a more holistic way than before. To investigate what has been referred to as "critical spatial practice," its vocabulary must first be described. The notion of "practice" already has many possible interpretations.

The term "spatial" is often understood to describe something that happens in space. However, within the context of spatial practice, its scope is far more concrete. In this context, spatial means something that not only happens in three-dimensional space but also has a certain effect on space, such as a policy or other legal or nonlegal framework. Something that is spatial always has an underlying structure to it, something that allows it to exist, that governs it formally or informally, a core that produces a setting for a condition and situation. Spatiality, in this regard, should be understood as a set of relations among humans, "things," and (built) structures—the built environment. It is this relationality embedded in the term that makes it political. Hence, political interventions are, by default, interventions in spatiality—that is, in relations rather than what is generally understood as "architecture." This force field of relations, according to architect and researcher Eyal Weizman, is "not only a neutral, abstract grid [...] but itself a dynamic and elastic territory [...] that is shaped by but also shapes conflict."[2]

The most indeterminate component of the triad term discussed here is "critical," which refers to when a person interrogates an existing practice or protocol and consequently maps out how to proactively alter, bastardize, augment, or develop this existing reality. In order to reach a decision, one first needs to gather information—studying, evaluating, and understanding the potential decision's repercussions. To decide entails forming conclusive thoughts, even if they are only temporary. When we are critical, we make a judgment, we determine which route to take. Sometimes such decision-making can be simple, though it is most often complex and requires a long and careful process of reading a situation, analysis, or dispute. But who validates this criticality? Who is in a position to determine and filter the critical?

The "critical" in critical spatial practice needs to be understood as an operative concept. There is a plethora of approaches that comes to mind when considering spatial practice and the practitioners who have informed it since the 1980s—when the notion of everyday practices, the production of space, time codes as complex social and spatial constructions, and the exploration of interdisciplinary intersections were investigated by protagonists such as Michel de Certeau and Henri Lefebvre. In the context of a relatively conventional understanding of architecture and urbanism, such theories—which stressed the productive activity inherent in everyday practices—caused huge debate, as many architects tend to concentrate on imaging, designing, and delivering stable conditions of certainty while often not considering the social and political consequences of their work. In the context of such a normative practice, bringing the everyday to the fore threatened a practice based on designing certainty.

While Lefebvre often wrote about the social relations of and within the processes of spatial production, de Certeau constructed an important distinction in the realm of spatial practices between "strategies" and "tactics." According to him, strategies are intrinsically produced by and located within institutional frameworks, propelled by the reified power structures and environments that they constitute, whereas tactics are employed by individuals who act within the actualities of territorial

Studio Miessen, Discursive Sauna, Artsonje Center,
Seoul, South Korea, 2014. Facade artwork by Liam Gillick

environments and sociopolitical force fields defined by the aforementioned institutions.

Critical spatial practice is interested in the *condition* of something—to alter the condition(s) that one encounters in the everyday. As opposed to traditional or normative architectural practices, which are mostly concerned with generating new designs and physical additions, spatial practice more frequently engages with acts of subtraction and revision: the alteration of conditions, which thus tweaks the very parameters of their existence. Spatial practice does not attempt to set itself apart from architecture or urbanism in a necessarily antagonistic way but simply offers and projects a more complex alternative in terms of its own approach to a given situation. In this way, it also proposes and promotes a more agonistic form of practice, one that values and nurtures the coexistence of different approaches and potentially conflictual beliefs in a common *space*.

The setting up of such scaffolding and meaning for practice implies that each individual contributor to a project needs to take a position, which always has consequences. Only when a border—a clearly distinguishable field of operation—is acknowledged can it be broken, transgressed, worked against, or (mis)-used. By deliberately producing such agonistic fields of encounter, critical spatial practice nurtures and exploits misunderstandings and a proactive outlook on the value of failure as a starting point for experimentation. Investigating the field's recent history, there have been countless projects that deal with complex narratives of "the political" within "the spatial," narratives around political congregation and the question of what constitutes "a" or "the" space for and of politics, and what I would like to refer to as "cultures of assembly."

Using the productive conflict between consensual and dissensual modes of practice as a driving force to

Markus Miessen, Ralf Pflugfelder, and Magnus Nilsson, Gwangju Biennial On Site, community hub for content production, 2011

Markus Miessen, Ralf Pflugfelder, and Magnus Nilsson, Backbench, Manifesta 8, Murcia, Spain, 2010

develop individual projects, critical spatial practice tends to think through the terms of "curating content" and "staging conflict" in order to develop methodologies as well as tools that help define socio-spatial frameworks that can be tested against reality—ranging from transient and informal to highly structured and formal. These changes in scale (physical) and intention ([in]-formalities) produce fertile grounds for speculation: If physical space (design) does not, at times, matter, what constitutes the elementary components of a spatial condition? Does decision-making take place only within the designed rigidity of the courtroom and the parliament, or does it also emerge in the informal corner of the corridor, between meetings, with coffee and a cigarette? And, if so, how can such processes or spaces be addressed through design?

We are currently, as we have been for the last fifteen years, experiencing a point of transition within participatory practices: within politics, within the Left, within spatial practices and—foremost—within architecture as their visible and most clearly defined product. Participation, both historically and in terms of political agency, is often read through romantic notions of negotiation, inclusion, and democratic decision-making. However, it is precisely this often unquestioned mode of inclusion that is used by populist politicians as a mode of campaigning. Hence it does not produce critical results, since criticality is being challenged by the conception of the majority. Instead, it will act as a catalyst for imagining a conflictual reading of participation as a mode of practice, one that opposes the consensus paradigm of the democratic facilitator; one that has to assume, at times, nonphysical violence and singular decision-making in order to produce frameworks for change. Imagine a conception of participation as a way to enter politics—proactively and consciously forcing us into existing power relations by intent—as opposed to a politically motivated model of participation, which tends to propose letting others contribute to the decision-making process. The latter, we might think, is habitually stirred by the craving for political legitimization. The former may be of interest not out of disbelief in democratic principles per se but out of sheer interest in critical and productive change. One could argue that this model inhabits a certain opportunism. It challenges the widespread default that majority equals judiciousness while arguing for a proactive citizenship in which the individual outsider to a given inbred political structure can become a driving force for change: forcefully entering an existing discourse rather than opening it up to the floor. Remaining within the arena of the democratic, let us instead bastardize participation into a form of nondemocratic practice, an opportunistic model of interventionism, in which interference is made possible owing to the fact that existing protocols of internalized political struggle are no longer followed. What is the alternative to a conventional confrontation based on the nostalgic notion of the barricade? How can one propose an alternative, embedded practice engaging in spatial projects dealing with social and political realities? What could such polyphonic practice potentially be? I would like to introduce such practice as "crossbenching."

Crossbenching delivers a contemporary and critical take on inclusiveness and, more concretely, on the way in which we (spatially) organize today as "publics." How do we gather, physically or virtually, and where and when? How are matters of urgency being discussed today, and what constitutes a democratic setting? Spatial planning is often considered as the management of spatial conflicts. The city—and indeed, the progressive institution—exists as a social and spatial conflict zone, renegotiating its limits through

Studio Missen, Performa Hub, Performa Biennial, New York, 2019, commissioned by RoseLee Goldberg

constant transformation. To deal with conflicts, critical decision-making must evolve. Such decision-making is often presupposed as a process whose ultimate goal is consensus. Opposing the politics of consensus, critical spatial practice shall foster micropolitical participation in the production of space, and ask the question of how one can contribute to alien fields of knowledge, professions, or discourses from the point of view of "space." Like the original meaning of the Latin word *conflictus* (fight), spatial conflict represents a clash of interests in using space. The future spatial practitioner could be understood as an outsider who—instead of trying to set up or sustain common denominators of consensus—enters existing situations or projects by deliberately instigating embedded conflicts between delineated fields of knowledge. Instead of aiming for synchronization, this kind of model could be based on participation through critical distance and the conscious implementation of zones of conflict. Within such zones, one could imagine the dismantling of existing situations in order to strategically isolate components that could be (mis)used to create friction.

Crossbenching should be read as an open framework of departure. It may start to create the friction necessary to both stir debate and move practice forward. If this had a single objective, it would be to develop a common understanding of the point from which we can start to disagree: a theory of how to participate—without squinting at constituencies or voters but by instigating critical debate and, at best, change. There may be two arguments here, one polemical and the other conceptually constructive, both driven by pragmatic optimism and at times developed through concrete situations and projects, which Simon Critchley would call "situated universality."[3]

1 Chantal Mouffe, in Markus Miessen and Chantal Mouffe, *The Space of Agonism* (Berlin: Sternberg Press, 2012), 64.
2 Eyal Weizman, introduction to *Forensis*, ed. Forensic Architecture (Berlin: Sternberg Press, 2014), 9.
3 Simon Critchley, *Infinitely Demanding: Ethics of Commitment, Politics of Resistance* (London: Verso, 2007), 42.

The Everyday through the Lens

Ciro Miguel

Montreux Gare
204 205 206

CLEANERS
PARKING
JEROME PARKING
1985 JEROME AVE. CORP.
OPEN 24 HRS
CARS CAP # 54
LIC. # 1421366
TEL. 716.7170
CARS, CAPACITY 54
ENTER 6:00 A.M. TO 6:00 P.M.
UP TO 12 HRS $ 8.00
UP TO 24 HRS $ 15.00
VAN $ 15.00
MONTHLY $ 200.00
MINI VAN SUV $ 15.00
NIGHT RATE
CARS, CAPACITY 54
ENTER 6:00 PM TO 6:00 AM
UP TO 12 HRS $ 10.00
UP TO 24 HRS $ 15.00
MONTHLY CARS $ 225.00
MINI VAN SUV $ 15.00
LARGE VAN $ 20.00
VAN MONTHLY $ 300.00
DEJAR LAS LLAVE DEL VEHICULO
PAY YOU MONTHLY RATE ON TIME
WE NOT RESPONSIBLE FOR LOST
OF ANY ARTICLES OR PERSONAL
PROP LEFT IN CARS UNLESS CHECK
NO SOMOS RESPONSABLE
POR NINGUN ARTICULO DEJADO
EN EL VEHICULO SIN ANTES HABERLO
INFORMADO A LA ADMINISTRACION
FAVOR REMOVER ARTICULOS DE VALOR
NOTICE
REGISTERED
No 1421366
State of New York
PARKING
1985 Jerome Ave.
BICYCLE PLACING
5 BIKES MAX
Coca-Cola

50

Sesc

IGREJA

Viaduto Santa Ifigênia, São Paulo, 2019
Bus stop, Montreux, 2020
Roman Forum, Rome, 2016
Parking lot, New York City, 2016
Avenida Paulista, São Paulo, 2019
Sesc Pompéia, São Paulo, 2019
Sesc 24 de Maio, São Paulo, 2019
Sesc 24 de Maio, São Paulo, 2019
Urban void after demolition, São Paulo, 2019
Ibirapuera Park's Marquise, São Paulo, 2019
Palace of Culture and Science, Warsaw, 2015
Copan Building, São Paulo, 2019
Casa de Vidro, São Paulo, 2019
Villa "Le Lac," Vevey, 2020
Sesc 24 de Maio, São Paulo, 2019

Jean-Baptiste Debret, "Végéteaux qui servent à faire des liens: Imbire (Cipò imbé), Cotonnier (Sapoucaÿa)," prints, 1834–39

Intervention of Another Nature: Resources for Thinking in (and out of) the Anthropocene

Renzo Taddei

Humans are hardwired to operate through narratives and fabulations, not to think about things or facts. Narratives are not only ideational; they are performative, entangled with materials, systems, mechanisms, algorithms, and affects. Every narrative entails diverse forms of intervention. One only has to consider narratives like liberalism or communism and think of the scale and complexity of the interventions they have generated.

Nature, resources, and the Anthropocene are three critical fabulations of our time. They are deeply interconnected in ways that are multiple and not easy to understand—the most elementary, perhaps, being the idea that the Anthropocene is the negative result of treating nature as an economic resource.

Anthropocene is the name that was suggested by Paul Crutzen and Eugene Stoermer in 2000 to describe the current geological epoch of the planet.[1] In 2019, the name was approved by the International Commission on Stratigraphy of the International Union of Geological Sciences. As of 2021 the concept has not yet been incorporated into the geological canon, but for years it has been part of debates in the environmental sciences, the social sciences, and the humanities. The epoch's designation comes from the scientific evidence that there are traces of human interference in all planetary ecosystems and organisms. These traces are multiple and diverse—for example, all life-forms with bones and teeth have radioactive levels in their organisms reflecting the military nuclear activity of the twentieth century. Furthermore, all ecosystems are polluted with plastics and microplastics, which are carried by the wind and have become part of the chemical composition of rain and water (and therefore of organisms that ingest this water) throughout the globe, even in the most remote and isolated areas. Per year human activity moves more sediment globally than all river basins. These indicators and many others will be part of the geological strata identified as having formed during the twentieth century or later.

When Nature Becomes a Resource

According to the proposition of the International Commission on Stratigraphy, the Anthropocene follows the Holocene, the epoch that began around twelve thousand years ago with the end of the last glaciation and ended with the atomic-weapons experiments of the mid-twentieth century. The Holocene's most distinctive quality is that the variation in climatic patterns was more stable than in previous epochs. This exceptional level of stability greatly affected human production; everything that we call civilization, philosophy, politics, and religion was created during the Holocene. This environmental stability led some peoples to the perception that nature was nothing more than the background or stage for human action.

The idea that nature is a pool of resources readily available for human exploitation originates in the transitional moment when humans shifted from nomadic hunting and gathering to agriculture, particularly in the Middle East. In a period of some four thousand years, this idea traveled from the mythologies of the populations of the Fertile Crescent to the sacred texts of Judaism and Christianity to reach the ideological paradigms of the Enlightenment and, finally, modern developmentalism.

An essential moment in the history of the idea of nature as a resource is tied to the expansion of Roman Catholicism across Europe, especially its aspect of imperialistic Platonism. It expelled spirits and deities from forests, rivers, mountains, and seas. Despiritualized, all these things became "empty spaces" first, and then "materials" conveniently used by the Industrial Revolution many centuries later.

The End of the Illusion of Absolute Knowledge

The Anthropocene is the epoch in which the aggregate human intervention in the Earth system knocks it out of thermodynamic balance, disturbing the environmental stability that marked the Holocene. Among its most visible manifestations are the accelerated melting of the polar caps and glaciers, the rise in average global temperature, the change in historical weather patterns, the rise of sea levels, the

Jean-Baptiste Debret, “Forêt vierge: Les Bords du Parahiba,”
print, 1834–39

transformation of ecosystems at such a dramatic pace as to cause massive extinction of plants and animals, and the disruption of patterns of relations between humans and other forms of life, generating, among many other things, cyclical pandemics. Nature moved from the background to center stage.[2]

The most important dimension of the Anthropocene, nevertheless, is not what is clearly available to human reason. The easiest and perhaps most psychologically comfortable way to think about the Anthropocene is to focus on its dimension of *mechanical* intervention: man becoming a geological power. There is a speck of hidden vanity in this fixation on human material pervasiveness. It is, perhaps, the survival of the feeling of human superiority, which now expresses itself in the form of melancholy.

However, it would be more instructive, and even more responsible, to focus on the Anthropocene as the moment of realization that the dominant narratives of reality—"modern" or "Western"—were wrong about their powers of knowledge. Humans, as all other living beings, can only perceive fragments of reality; they then glue these pieces together with the sticky power of paradigms and ideologies. But paradigms and ideologies, despite often presenting themselves as universal and atemporal, have the sole function of enabling agendas to move forward, and are therefore limited in scope, time, and space. The Anthropocene is the moment when the global elites (cultural and scientific ones included) realize that their paradigms and ideologies were efficacious in helping them accomplish their short-term desires, but at the price of destroying everyone's capacity for long-term survival.

It is terribly difficult to admit that most of those identified with the West fell prey to the illusion of absolute Knowledge to dissuade them from the idea that Nature, in its most transcendental interpretation, would open up to them and give them divine powers. The pain brought about by the Anthropocene is related to the fact that the current crises force Westerners to face their incapacity to perceive and make sense of the aggregate effects of their actions outside of the microscopic scale the human mind can effectively handle.

Modern civilization will not be able to rise to the challenge if it fails to question its own conceptual paradigms. We know from the reports of the Intergovernmental Panel on Climate Change, which are often considered conservative, that if the Earth system reaches certain tipping points, chains of events may happen abruptly, and the impacts on ecosystems may be so intense that tropical forests transform into savannahs, savannahs into semiarid areas, and semiarid areas into deserts. One likely planetary impact of such transformation is the creation of unimaginably large waves of migration from the globe's equatorial belt to higher latitudes. This would probably be exponentially larger than what caused the immigration crisis of the last decade in Europe—and it may also make the nation-state system, based as it is on the control of sovereign borders, collapse.

New Conceptual Tools, from the Planet's Fringes

The fact is that we might not have the conceptual tools to make sense of this crisis.[3] If the sciences fail to easily recognize the problem, the arts, as a form of contemporary mythology, clearly acknowledges it. The end of the world became a dominant theme in the fabulations of the West; utopian fantasies for the future disappeared from stages and movie theaters. Under these circumstances, Fredric Jameson's famous phrase "It is more difficult to think about the end of capitalism than about the end of the world" gains a new, more interesting meaning.[4] Most people understand the end of Western models of social order and governance as the end of what is meaningful. This is the negative side effect of having made Enlightenment subjectivity the model for what it is to be human. What does not reflect the self is perceived as chaos.

This is the moment in which we perceive noise coming from the fringes of reality. From the struggles of the excluded minorities a message is delivered: what the West calls "the end of the world" is, perhaps, a lack of imagination more than anything else. Our capacity for imagining alternative realities may in fact have been severely damaged by the Enlightenment. For the Indigenous peoples of the Americas, for instance, the end of the world began in 1492,[5] and survival outside of capitalism has been an everyday ongoing project ever since.

If the knowledge regimes of the West fail to make sense of the current challenges, we should pay attention to other forms of knowing and thinking, for we may learn from people whose lives are affected by disasters of our own making. In this current panorama, Indigenous ways of being may become radical and interesting forms of intervention. In fact, interest in the modes of existence of Indigenous populations is on the rise. Some of these populations thrived in the heart of the planet's most abundant sources of material resources—tropical forests such as the Amazon—while promoting biodiversity and keeping a low carbon footprint. That is precisely where we want to be in the future.

Most people compare themselves to others using the dimensions of life in which they are successful, in their own view—Westerners and Westernized individuals measure their accomplishments through material accumulation (even if expressed indirectly, through things like amount of concrete or amount of bytes) and feel appalled when they are compared to Indigenous populations. This is a symptom of the problem, naturally; this kind of association of ideas often produces nonsense in contexts of intercultural contact. A more relevant comparison, I would argue, is related to how forms of knowing precipitate and reflect forms of being and forms of relating to others—and the implications they have for what we call "the environment."

Nature as Kinship, Knowledge as Care

Because of the work of Indigenous thinkers like Davi Kopenawa and Amazonian ethnologists, we know that the Amerindian world is composed of different perspectives about reality, of which the human is just one. Among these considerations is the belief that no one is superior to others, and that in normal conditions, one type of being (humans, for instance) cannot access the perspective of another (such as jaguars or tapirs). Reality is defined by perspective: what is blood for humans is manioc beer for jaguars, and one alternative is not truer or more real than the other.[6] Animals have intentionality—that is, they are subjects—in ways that are akin to humans; their different bodies, which define different perspectives, prevent these subjectivities from interacting directly with each other. This means that the human by definition cannot know the world of the jaguar. Shamans play a special role here: in certain circumstances, they may cross the border of species and catch a glimpse of the world of jaguars. Since jaguars are subjects, the shaman does not connect to the world of jaguars, or of tapirs, out of curiosity or to catalogue the existing worlds. He does it as a strategy to try to manage the coexistence of beings that are epistemologically disconnected while ontologically linked through the bondage of prey–predator relations. In

Jean-Baptiste Debret, "Cocotier barrigudo (ventrû),"
print, 1834–39

short, shamans have the critical task of administering matters of life and death that they, by definition, cannot fully understand. Under these circumstances, every act of knowing is, first and foremost, an act of care.

It is important to understand that, in a place where everything is potentially a subject, nature does not exist. In the most important aspects of life, humans do not interact with matter but with beings with (or linked to some form of) intentionality. This applies to animals but also to rivers, mountains, forests, and the atmosphere. Relations with these beings are, therefore, social, and as such they are guided by strict moral codes.

All this is schematic and oversimplified, of course. But some of these things are at the core of what the Indigenous peoples of the Americas have been telling settlers for five centuries.[7] From the perspective of these peoples, the European settlers and their (epistemological) descendants have behaved, all this time, as irresponsible, arrogant wealthy youngsters who believe anything can be done without fear of consequence because of the powerful father who will always fix the situation. The powerful father sometimes is evoked as the God who created all creatures for human exploitation, sometimes as a Nature that has infinite capacity for absorbing blows, and sometimes as a metaphysical Progress that will solve the future problems caused by humans in the past and the present. The Anthropocene is the painful realization that there is no father. Perhaps a more productive understanding of what the Anthropocene is portrays it as an immense rite of passage. One that is inevitably painful, with Dantesque amounts of suffering and no justice, but that will produce mature adults responsible for their actions.

In societal terms, one important message of Indigenous philosophies is that care has precedence over knowing, or that knowing is only legitimate if it is a dimension of care, in the most pragmatic of senses. Leaders like Kopenawa are tired of seeing armies of scientists studying the Amazon with ever increasing intensity, which in practical terms rarely produces real protection of the forest.[8] Never before has science known so much about the forest, and never before has the forest been attacked and destroyed with the intensity it is now. If knowing is not an integral part of caring, it is hubris and foolishness.

Geo-biological Equity

Hope comes from the noise emanating from another unexpected source: the fringes of science itself. A silent revolution seems to be taking place inside of the walls of academia. From neuroscience, we know that mammals, birds, and other creatures like octopuses have the physiological features required to produce consciousness. Animal studies have shown us that mammals understand and react to unfairness, demonstrating a capacity for moral reasoning we did not know existed. Monkeys, dolphins, and whales can invent creative solutions to problems and teach them to their offspring—which qualifies as "culture" as we understand it. Dolphins and whales use proper names in their communication. Some monkeys can purposefully change the "system of government" of their band. Trees communicate with each other through networks of fungi that have been called "the Internet of plants"; senior trees seem to take care, chemically, of youngsters.[9] From biology, we now understand that cooperation among organisms and species is much more prevalent and important than what the Darwinian paradigm suggested, and symbiosis goes way beyond what we might understand as "cooperation." In many cases, what we call an "organism" is rather a dynamic composite in which life itself is dependent on

Jean-Baptiste Debret, "Vallée da Serra do Mar (Chaine de montaignes près de la mer)," print, 1834–39

the coexistence of individuals of different species.[10] Humans are the most distinctive case in point: no life is possible without a healthy gut microbiome formed by organisms that do not share DNA with the rest of the body. This same microbiome has an important role in the production of chemicals in the human body that regulate the functioning of the nervous system, affecting patterns of thinking and emotions. Other varieties of microbiome are crucial for the proper functioning of the human immune system.

All these factors have resulted in nature gaining rights that are equivalent to those of humans in the constitutions of Ecuador and Bolivia and rivers gaining equivalent rights in New Zealand. In India, dolphins were declared "nonhuman persons" and all aquariums with cetaceans were banned. A few years ago, animal-rights activists started a global campaign against cruelty to great apes, and in different countries a concerted effort called for habeas corpus for zoo chimpanzees, with some victories. In fact, a recent analysis of the DNA of humans and chimpanzees arrived at 98.8 percent similarity, which led some scientists to call for the reclassification of chimps inside of the genus *Homo* (that is, as another kind of human).[11]

All this could be an extraordinary—indeed, sensational—arch that bends Western knowledge of reality in directions that point to unequivocal similarities with Indigenous philosophies. However, we should be careful not to fall, once more, into the self-indulgent trap of the myth of absolute knowledge. The message from Indigenous philosophies must be repeated: if it does not lead to the construction of relations of care, knowledge is equivalent to nothing. New forms of intervention, then, are desperately needed—interventions of another nature. We need to construct strategies and mechanisms for the scaling up of modes of existence in which knowledge and care are indistinguishable, no matter their origin.

Interventions of Another Nature

We need to nudge ourselves into collectivities in which any act of knowledge is also the promotion of what Kopenawa calls the "value of growth" (*në rope*, in the Yanomami language), which reproduces life in the forest. Architecture, urbanism, and design have a special role to play in this context in at least four particularly important dimensions. The first one refers to the work of mourning for the fabulations we need to abandon. It is difficult to leave behind such flattering (even if disastrous) images of ourselves. This must be done through new forms of experiencing reality.

The second is that we need to rethink how the many works of care are spatialized and temporalized into forms of experience in our societies. Care needs to break the disciplinary chains that associate it with a few restricted spaces (such as hospitals) and professions. We need to be ready to enact care in each and every social context. These social contexts may be designed, as much as possible, to facilitate care.

Third, issues associated with spatial organization at larger scales play a central role. If the nature–culture dichotomy is to be surpassed, how does that affect established forms of thinking about space, such as the urban/suburban/rural divide? New paradigms for spatial organization will not be based on presences and absences (of certain types of infrastructure, for instance) but on relations and their enactments.

And fourth, we need to realize that the construction of a planetary community will inevitably require humans to abandon specist tendencies. A global collectivity cannot be made solely of humans. The biosphere is infused with life and myriad forms of

Jean-Baptiste Debret, “Sauvages Goyanas
(À O Mar Pequeno),” print, 1834–39

consciousness connected through symbiotic relations that are important for planetary dynamic equilibrium, and some of these relations may be of predation. The idea that humans do not have predators is make-believe. Philosophically, it is crucial that humans deeply incorporate the idea that they have predators—the healthy functioning of the biosphere may require it. We take it as a blessing that we do not understand the environmental role played by viruses and the like so we can wage our total wars against them. We will eventually, perhaps with the help of artificial intelligence, detect and understand symbiotic relations across the biosphere in much richer detail and be able to comprehend that some things that kill us have important roles to play in the maintenance of the equilibrium of the whole. When that day arrives, we will need novel forms of understanding life and death, for the greater planetary good.

All images from Jean-Baptiste Debret, *Voyage pittoresque et historique au Brésil, ou Séjour d'un artiste français au Brésil depuis 1816 jusqu'en 1831 inclusivement* (Paris: Firmin Didot, 1834–39).

1 Paul J. Crutzen and Eugene F. Stoermer, "The 'Anthropocene,'" *Global Change Newsletter*, no. 41 (May 2000): 17–18.

2 Nature, the youngest actor in the political arena in 1970, when the environmental movement was born, became the very *condition of possibility* of politics. See Bruno Latour, *Facing Gaia: Eight Lectures on the New Climatic Regime*, trans. Catherine Porter (Hoboken, NJ: John Wiley & Sons, 2017).

3 Déborah Danowski and Eduardo Viveiros de Castro, *The Ends of the World*, trans. Rodrigo Guimaraes Nunes (Hoboken, NJ: John Wiley & Sons, 2017).

4 Mark Fisher, *Capitalist Realism: Is There No Alternative?* (London: Zero Books), 1.

5 Danowski and Viveiros de Castro, *Ends of the World*, 104.

6 Eduardo Viveiros de Castro, "Perspectival Anthropology and the Method of Controlled Equivocation," *Tipití* 2, no. 1 (2004): 1–22.

7 The message is reiterated, once more, by Yanomami shaman Davi Kopenawa. See Davi Kopenawa and Bruce Albert, *The Falling Sky: Words of a Yanomami Shaman*, trans. Nicholas Elliott and Alison Dundy (Cambridge, MA: Harvard University Press, 2013).

8 Renzo Taddei, "Kopenawa and Environmental Research in the Amazon," in *Philosophy on Fieldwork: Case Studies in Anthropological Analysis*, ed. Nils Bubandt and Thomas Schwarz Wentzer (London: Routledge, forthcoming).

9 Anna Lowenhaupt Tsing, *The Mushroom at the End of the World: On the Possibility of Life in Capitalist Ruins* (Princeton, NJ: Princeton University Press, 2015), 139.

10 Donna Haraway, *Staying with the Trouble: Making Kin in the Chthulucene* (Durham, NC: Duke University Press, 2016), 60.

11 Derek E. Wildman, Monica Uddin, Guozhen Liu, Lawrence I. Grossman, and Morris Goodman, "Implications of Natural Selection in Shaping 99.4% Nonsynonymous DNA Identity between Humans and Chimpanzees: Enlarging Genus *Homo*," *Proceedings of the National Academy of Sciences* 100, no. 12 (June 2013): 7181–88.12.

A Tale of Two Slates: On Collapse and Complicity

Caitlin DeSilvey

"This happened," read the brief email message from my husband. I clicked on the attachment and saw our front porch collapsed onto the path outside our home, surrounded by a scatter of broken slates and splintered wood. A slow, mostly invisible process of decay had reached its conclusion. The 125-year-old iron bolts had gradually oxidized; moisture had collected on the back sides of the wooden supports, against the damp granite; together, rot and rust worked away at their chemical and organic labors. When it came, the failure was sudden, and severe. The "happening" is the breach in the everyday, the swerve in which ordinary architecture is exposed in its vulnerability, belly-up, like a dead horse.

So, the story begins here, on the front path of a terraced granite cottage in a village in Cornwall, in the far southwest of England, in October 2019. But what happened next? This essay shares the rest of the tale, which is notably less dramatic and vivid than the initial event. As with most narratives of maintenance and repair, it is composed of a series of minor decisions, delays, and deliberations. It unfolds in stuttering stages, leaps forward, and long pauses. It ties in with other stories and other lives. It reveals, I'll suggest, something about *complicity*.

Beyond its most common definition, which implies some form of guilt by association, complicity is also defined more broadly as a "state of being complex or involved." Maintenance is not commonly understood as a particularly complex or involved practice. Things break and wear; we fix them. But, as other contributions in this book show, the process is never that simple. Maintenance always involves choices—about methods, materials, makers—and these choices are hitched indelibly to other subjectivities and other geographies. In this essay, I narrate this involvement and complexity to see where it leads us. The details, though they may seem banal and insignificant, are necessary, so bear with me.

Chapter 1

Our porch collapse coincides with the sudden unemployment of a friend. He's casting around for work, and comes over to take a look at our problem. We live in the middle of a row of three once-identical Victorian cottages built by the village doctor to house his offices, his own home, and the home of his elderly mother. The local museum has a photograph taken about a decade after construction that shows the trio with their matching porches and bay windows, marching down the hill. Over the years, the cottages have been altered to meet the tastes and needs of their subsequent owners, but the porches remained original and intact until a few years ago, when the neighbors on

CORNISH ARMS
HOTEL

our downhill side decided to partly enclose their porch with side panels to keep out the prevailing westerlies. The break in the unity of the row is noticeable, and our recent collapse has broken the pattern completely. We decide in conversation with our friend that he will try to replicate the original design as faithfully as possible. He thinks he can probably salvage the carved diagonal supports and build them into a new frame. He quotes us a reasonable price for the job and comes around with his father-in-law's pickup truck to haul the carcass back to his workshop. He sends us an update a week later, reporting that the work is going well, and that he's sourced a stock of cheap modern slate from a supplier in a nearby village.

The next couple months are very wet. Our porchless door leaks rain onto the granite sill with every storm. We see our friend around and ask about his progress; he gestures at the sky. He explains that he needs a run of dry weather to set the epoxy on the new bolts that will anchor the structure into the stone wall. We receive an email on January 20 with the subject line: "high pressure!" He hangs the rebuilt frame the next week, setting it onto the steel bolts, and delivers a stack of grayish-green slate tiles, their texture smooth and even.

We have a chat about the slate installation, and the friend realizes that he hasn't calculated for an overhang on either side of the pitch. He makes up the difference by increasing the gap between each slate, nailing them onto the cladding boards quickly as dusk closes in on a January afternoon. In the light of the next morning, I notice that the line of the slates on the bottom of the pitch is off, hanging lower by an inch or two on one side. I wonder if I should say anything, and decide to send an email asking if he could reset them. He replies, "I did it by Cornish eye, not level should have checked what it looked like from your side not just the road side!" and offers to fix it. But the rain comes again, and it doesn't stop until March. We will later learn that February 2020 was England's wettest February on record since 1862.[1]

Chapter 2

On March 16, the sun breaks through the clouds, and our friend appears out front with a ladder. He removes the slates and stacks the unbroken ones in the front yard. That evening, Boris Johnson tells us to avoid all nonessential social contact and to work from home if possible. Lockdown officially begins a week later. The friend says that he needs a few more slates to finish the job and replace the broken ones, but in the first few weeks of lockdown the slate supplier isn't trading. When things start to open up again in late April, the friend says he's waiting for a rainy day to make the trip to collect what he needs. The rainy day doesn't come. The sun shines and shines and the exposed cladding boards begin to warp and split. May 2020 ranks as the driest May on record for England.[2]

In the middle of the month, a roofer begins work on our next-door neighbors' bay window. The slates he uses are smaller and more varied in texture than the ones stacked in our front yard. The roofer sets the tiles in a lime mortar onto wooden battens, his skill and care evident. I chat with him about what he is doing, and about our slate-less porch. In an attempt to restart our stalled job, I send a message to the friend offering to buy the slates he needs myself if he can find time to finish the work. He accepts the offer, and suggests that if he can't get to it maybe the roofer (whom he knows) can do the work as a favor to him, since he's already essentially on-site. I correspond with the local supplier, sending him photos of the new slates so he can match them. He replies: "I believe they are 400 x 200mm Brazilian Grey/Green slate."

The roofer says that he has an account with the supplier and that he can source what's needed, but he seems reluctant to commit to the job. Eventually, it becomes clear that he would prefer not to use the Brazilian slates. He offers to use reclaimed Cornish slates instead, like the ones he used next door. He gives me a quote for the work and I accept it. He texts back: "I will be happy to lay Cornish slates to your porch. More appropriate for the village and a more durable job." He explains that he'll be using slate tiles salvaged from the roof of a farmhouse on the other side of the river, which he has sorted and cleaned. He does the job over two days in early June, leaving the final priming and painting to me. I ask if he wants to take the unused Brazilian slates for another job, and he says he'd rather not. He doesn't like working with them because they tend to shatter when they are cut rather than cleave as ordinary slates do.

Chapter 3

A week or so later, in the middle of June, on my way into my writing studio in the nearby town, I notice a pallet of slate tiles sitting outside the back door in the rain. A plastic label on the pallet says "Made in Brazil," and the slates resemble those left behind in my front yard. The granite building that houses my studio is a former school, built in three stages between 1897 and 1913, and the roof is a rambling range of pitches and slopes, all clad in the original Cornish slates, now fragile and failing in places. The next day I have a chat with the man who is doing the roofing work.

He prefers Spanish slates, he explains, but the Brazilian ones are cheap, at around forty pence a tile. Spanish slate is at least twenty pence more, hard to afford on a big job. I ask him about using Cornish slate and he raises his eyebrows: "Too dear, and there is a

WESTLAND GREY GREEN
CE

waiting list." He implies that the Cornish slate industry, based fifty miles away in Delabole, now focuses on high-end clients. I ask what will happen with the old tiles, and he says that they will likely get crushed and used as fill. "A lot of them are knackered," he explains, and break when you pull the nails used to fasten them. He's been asked to set aside the undamaged tiles for reuse on one on the outbuildings, and a small stack is building up on the scaffolding. He speculates that the original slate could have come from Delabole, or maybe from Wales. It looks very similar to the reclaimed slate just installed on our porch roof.

I take a photograph of one of the pallet labels with details of provenance and certification of the new slate: "Location of the mine/quarry: Pompéu, Brazil." A brief online search places Pompéu in Brazil's state Minas Gerais, which loosely translates as "General Mines." The state is dominated by extractive industries and notorious for two recent catastrophic dam collapses associated with the Vale mining company, one on the Paraopeba River upstream of the town of Pompéu. Through correspondence with a Brazilian colleague, and translation assistance from a Portuguese friend, I learn that Pompéu lies in a dedicated "slate province" (*Província de Ardósia*), where the material is abundant, accessible, and easily extracted.[3] Recent investment has focused on building up international markets, and Brazilian slate has become popular in the United Kingdom because it is inexpensive and remarkably uniform in quality and texture. Apparently, some Brazilian slate is classed as sedimentary mudstone rather than true metamorphic slate, which gives it different properties when worked and a tendency to absorb moisture when installed (though the certification on the pallet would suggest otherwise for this particular batch).

Where does this story leave us? Somewhere between Cornwall and Brazil, between COVID-19 and climate change, stuck in a tale of two slates. I've narrated the essential details: a porch fails; nine months later, its repair is complete. A simple story, really; or not, depending on how you want to cut it. On the subject of "cutting," in the course of writing this piece I learned that in a true slate the process of metamorphosis involves the application of sustained low-grade pressure or heat, which transforms mudstone or shale deposits by realigning their mineral structure into new planes, creating a harder stone with schistose foliation. The resulting slate splits, or cleaves, along these new planes. If this metamorphic process does not take place, softer mudstone or shale will split along the original bedding planes, making it easier to extract but also less durable.

Maybe societies are like slates: subject to unexpected impact, they break along new planes of possibility, learning from past pressures, or they reveal themselves as weak and brittle, prone to shattering. Our world at the moment is cut through with crises, but the effects of these crises are not being felt evenly.[4] Climate breakdown and global contagion play out in major and minor ways, in specific places and processes, and in everyday stories about, in this case, failed maintenance, eventual collapse, and incremental repair. I did not choose to purchase the Brazilian slates for the roof of my porch or the roof of the building I write this in, but I am still complicit in the act of their extraction far away in the slate mines of Minas Gerais. I can choose whether to translate this complicity into indifference or into connection. To "cleave" can mean to split apart, its roots in the Germanic word for "cloven" (as in hooves). Or it can have an entirely opposite meaning: to adhere, to "cleave" one thing onto another.

If, as I argued in *Curated Decay*, we need to rethink our care of historic architectures to adopt an ethical stance that allows us to collaborate with—rather than defend against—natural processes, perhaps a theory of relational complicity is a corollary to this practice.[5] In some instances, faced with the disintegration and transformation of material fabric, the most ethically sound position is to do very little, and to observe the emergence of novel ecologies and other-than-human communities. When this is not feasible, and when intervention is necessary (as with a collapsed front porch, or, arguably, a clouded glass facade) we need to be aware of how every choice, however apparently minor, binds us to other people, and other landscapes, in complex and indelible relationships. Such relationships remain, for the most part, invisible in our maintenance of everyday architectures. A methodology oriented to the telling of incidental stories of how buildings come together, and come apart, is perhaps our best tool in repairing this blindness.

Image on page 145 reproduced with permission of the Museum of Cornish Life, Helston, Cornwall, reference: HESFM_2002_8042_2_2048_c 1904_Helston Museum.jpg. Other images are by the author and Russell Johnston.

1 Mark McCarthy, "Met Office: Why the UK Saw Record-Breaking Rainfall in February 2020," *Carbon Brief*, March 5, 2020, https://www.carbonbrief.org/met-office-why-the-uk-saw-record-breaking-rainfall-in-february-2020.

2 Annie Schultz and Ayesha Tandon, "Met Office: Why 2020 Saw a Record-Breaking Dry and Sunny Spring across the UK," *Carbon Brief*, June 4, 2020, https://www.carbonbrief.org/met-office-why-2020-saw-a-record-breaking-dry-and-sunny-spring-across-the-uk.

3 Walter Francisco Figueiredo Lowande, a historian at the Universidade Federal de Alfenas in Minas Gerais, kindly shared his knowledge about the extraction of slate in Brazil. Catarina Fontoura provided additional translation assistance.

4 See, for instance, Delaney Murray, "Pandemic and Persecution: The Double Threat Facing Brazil's Indigenous," *Globe Post*, August 26, 2020, https://theglobepost.com/2020/08/24/threats-brazil-indigenous/.

5 Caitlin DeSilvey, *Curated Decay: Heritage beyond Saving* (Minneapolis: University of Minnesota Press, 2017).

AQUI TEM

Architecture as Ultra-clear Rendered Society

Andrés Jaque
(Office for Political Innovation)

Gerson Santos Nascimento lives in Jardim João XXIII, a neighborhood in the Raposo Tavares district of western São Paulo.[1] It takes him two and a half hours to commute by public bus to Serviço Social do Comércio (Sesc) 24 de Maio in central São Paulo.

He arrives at Sesc at 2:00 pm and works for eight hours.

He works for the maintenance company Grupo RCA in labor outsourcing. He is responsible for keeping the facades of the building clean.

This requires permanent dedication because of the high level of atmospheric pollution in the city. The architectural component that is most difficult to clean is the building's clear glass facade.

Traffic-related carbon dioxide and nitrogen oxide in the air precipitate on the surface of the clear glass, making it lose its transparency.

Since the clear glass is one of the most esteemed architectural features of the building, Gerson's work is fundamental in keeping the building's performance aligned with its architects' intentions.

Through the clarity of its material, the building's glazed facade conveys a visual sense of permeability with the street, even though it is in fact quite a hermetic envelope.

This complicates Gerson's work.

He needs to find a way to reach each point of the facade's exterior through a very limited number of openings.

The capacity for the building to keep performing in the way its architects envisioned requires a long list of cleaning routines that Gerson honors every week.

In 2017, Sesc, a nonprofit institution supported by private capital, opened a new branch in central São Paulo: Sesc 24 de Maio.[2]

It was designed by Pritzker-winning architect Paulo Mendes da Rocha together with the architect Milton Braga.

The main purpose of the architectural design is to provide São Paulo's citizens with a very particular notion of societal transparency.

According to Mendes da Rocha: "It is the transparency that is experienced when you

are doing an activity inside a space in the heart of the city, like dancing, when a process of interlocution is established. The building puts on a show. A sequence of rooms and actions played in relationship with the street. […] In São Paulo, more than a million people travel to the center everyday. In Sesc the whole interior activity is exposed to the street."[3]

And this is the reason why the clear-glass facade is such an important element in the architecture of the building. It is intended to expose its interior life to a street system that is occupied every day by a million people like Gerson who commute to central São Paulo from peripheral urban locations.

The architects took this aim for clarity to the material definition of the facade's construction.[4]

They planned it to be constructed out of Ultra Clear Glass.[5]

A type of glass capable of preserving both an exceptional level of colorless transparency and a significant solar factor, which results in a reduction of the heat transmitted to the interior.[6]

Through a conflicted design process that faced budget adjustments over a period of several years, the main financial focus ended up being the fifth facade of the swimming-pool rooftop area.

The glazed facade was never planned to be green.

The preference for colorless Ultra Clear Glass was abandoned because of its cost. A more economical option, floated glass with high contents of iron oxide, was finally installed. It gave the facade a green coloration and a high mirrorlike reflectivity, which did not align with the initial priorities expressed by the architects.[7]

In 1989, PPG Industries patented Starphire, the first industrially produced low-iron floated glass.[8]

A surprisingly clear glass that rapidly became a desired architectural component and an indicator of global financial power.

By 2008, four transnational corporate giants—Saint Gobain, Guardian Glass, Pilkington, and AGC—had stabilized a steady 6 percent annual growth in the production of Ultra Clear Glass (UCG).[9]

With an annual production of 2,271,000 tons, the UCG industry will reach $5.1 billion in revenue by 2021.[10]

It is commercialized under brands such as Starphire, Diamant, Clearvision, Optiwhite, and AGC Clear.

UCG is composed of 73 percent SiO2, 14 percent Na2O, 10 percent CaO, and 3 percent MgO and trace elements.[11]

With an iron content below 0.01 percent (ten times less than ordinary glass), UCG reaches up to 97 percent of light transmittance, avoiding the greenish tone that characterizes ordinary glass.[12]

The colorless quality of UCG increases its compatibility with an exceptionally broad range of radiation-filtering coatings, allowing a very selective management of the amount of energy contained in the incoming

STARPHIRE
ULTRA-CLEAR GLASS

CLEAR GLASS

and outgoing radiation of a building. This capacity makes UCG the best-performing clear panel used to engineer the transmittance of incoming and outgoing radiation in buildings with glass envelopes.[13]

Sold as the top premium product of the glass industry, the price of UCG is at least 30 percent higher than any standard clear glass.[14]

Exceptional clarity.

Optimum transparency.

Unfiltered natural light.

Unrestricted views.

Colorless appearance.

Purity of color.

These are the commonplace slogans used to advertise UCG worldwide.

The presence of iron oxide raises the melting point at which silica sand becomes the incandescent mass out of which clear glass is produced.

Iron oxide helps shorten the process of cooling the glass in the tin bath.

The production of UCG requires the removal of iron oxide when the silica sand is mixed in.

This increases the energy required to melt the mix by 30 percent, which, together with a 100 percent increase in the energy required to slow down the process of cooling, more than doubles the energy required to make mullions floating in the air.

Seventy-three percent of the energy fueling the production of UCG comes from natural gas.[15] In the United States, the increase of energy consumption that UCG has brought to the built environment is fueled by the natural gas extracted by hydraulic fracturing, or fracking.

As an associated effect of the energy-efficient performance of coated UCG installed in high-end buildings branded as green in cities all around the globe, rural locations like Toledo, Ohio, and Wedron, Illinois, are experiencing a radical increase in the atmospheric concentration of carbon dioxide and nitrogen oxides.

The production of low-iron glass requires the use of silica sand with an almost nonexistent content of iron oxide as a raw material.

Companies providing "high-quality low-iron silica sand" worldwide such as Fairmount Santrol or US Silica concentrate their production in the United States in the states of Illinois and Wisconsin.[16] The product is known as St. Peter Sandstone.[17]

The growth of surface mining of St. Peter Sandstone has been boosted by an increase in the demand from both the UCG and the fracking industries.[18]

The volatility of the sand led to the pollution of farmland and water bodies in the region and a non-scrutinized exponential growth of lung-affecting diseases such as silicosis and carcinoma.[19]

Susquehanna Valley is a rural area in Pennsylvania where the natural gas that fuels UCG production is extracted from the Marcellus Shale through fracking.

As a result, 36,000 river miles in Susquehanna Valley now jeopardize human and animal life because of the high concentration of pollutants associated with the fracking industry.

LEED, or Leadership in Energy and Environmental Design, is the most widely used green-building rating system in the world.

Even though the production of a ton of Starphire glass requires 40 percent more carbon dioxide, 400 percent more sulfur dioxide, and 400 percent more ozone emissions than a ton of Portland cement, when rating a specific building, two points are automatically earned when UCG is installed, as UCG products have an LEED-verified environmental product declaration.[20]

Ultra Clear Glass is not just a construction solution but a socio-territorial apparatus intended to segregate humans and nonhumans in zones of diverse levels of pollution exposure.

The effect of being exposed to São Paulo's pollution is equivalent to smoking four cigarettes a day. The levels of pollutants such as nitrous dioxide caused by so-called commuter trips, which involve people like Gerson traveling to the city center from peripheral neighborhoods, concentrate in the central area of the city, where most of these trips either end or start.[21]

A significant number of people working in São Paulo require daily commutes that exceed six hours.

In a city where most work opportunities are concentrated in the center, a congested mobility system—where helicopters, apps like

Uber, private cars, and a complex network of privately managed buses coexist—becomes a sorting device for societies in segregated consumption niches.[22]

In this ecosystem, the life and experience of low-income commuters is highly affected by a specific feature of the transit system:

Even though fares are momentous in the economy of franchised transportation companies, the companies heavily rely on the fleet of vehicles as an asset that can be sold to smaller cities.[23]

Normally, this happens after three years of use.

This makes it financially difficult for transportation companies to move into nonpolluting sources of energy, since it would complicate selling vehicles to companies operating in smaller cities.[24]

Even though the distribution of pollution in São Paulo has historically coincided with the concentration of work opportunities, the distribution of its effects on human health has depended on income.[25]

Those citizens of São Paulo with the lowest levels of income were the ones with the longest commutes, and were therefore exposed to air pollutants for a longer period of time.[26]

This has been Gerson's case. Commuting from Jardim João XXIII to São Paulo to make the Sesc's facade transparent by making pollution imperceptible requires him to be exposed to highly polluted air for two and a half hours daily.[27]

Higher rates of respiratory diseases are now found in sections of the population

5_17 - 10_41_43.PNG
SÃO PAULO
CAOS NO TRANSPORTE DE SP: 65 ÔNIBUS QUEBRAM POR DIA
23°
FROTA ANTIGA

VIA AV. PAULISTA
857R
Av. Paulista
Av. Rebouças
10
Av. Francisco Morato
EU DOU PREFERÊNCIA À VIDA.

with lower income, resulting in an unequal geography of life expectancy.[28]

In recent years, a series of policies was introduced that intended to reduce the problems of mobility in São Paulo's city center.[29]

Dozens of kilometers of car lanes were reserved for buses, reducing the emissions associated with public-transit commuting.[30]

According to Paulo Saldiva, a professor at the University of São Paulo and an expert in urban pollution, this initiative eventually led to an increase in the use of public transit among the population living in the city center.

The construction of bike lanes and more restrictive speed limits were implemented in the city center as the result of the city's partnership with Bloomberg Philanthropies, which helps develop plans to increase the environmental quality of affluent central areas of the city.[31]

Commuters from peripheral parts of the city still spend hours coming to central São Paulo every day to work.

A big part of their daily journey traverses highly polluted areas of the city that were not taken care of by Bloomberg Philanthropies' experts, in what seems to be a stimulation of the socio-territorial divide.

Transparency

In 1983, architectural theorists Colin Rowe and Robert Slutzky opened the debate on the notions of transparency that architecture enacted, and how visual transparency had been surpassed by the reality of architectural design.

Rowe and Slutzky quoted Gyorgy Kepes, who in 1944 had claimed: "Transparency […] implies more than an optical characteristic, it implies a broader spatial order. Transparency means a simultaneous perception of different spatial locations."[32]

An intervention in architecture's addiction to visual transparency is needed—as well as a call for architecture to care for the diverse and divided constituencies it convenes and affects.

This essay is a screenplay of a video installation conceived for the 12th International Architecture Biennale of São Paulo. Invited to intervene on the glass facade of Sesc 24 de Maio, one of the event's venues, Andrés Jaque (Office for Political Innovation) proposed *Architecture as Rendered Society*. To conceive this work, Jaque and his research team conducted a series of interviews with an interdisciplinary group of interlocutors, from the building's architects to its cleaners to prominent experts on São Paulo's urban and environmental issues. The video installation invited visitors and bystanders to reflect on how the most trivial aspects of construction can disclose deep and unknown political, economic, and social mechanisms.

All images are video stills taken from *Architecture as Rendered Society* (2019).

1 Gerson Nascimento, interview with Helena Cavalheiro and the author, August 2019.
2 Pedro Vada, “Sesc 24 de Maio / Paulo Mendes da Rocha + MMBB Arquitetos,” *Archdaily*, July 18, 2019, https://www.plataformaarquitectura.cl/cl/921448/sesc-24-de-maio-paulo-mendes-da-rocha-plus-mmbb-arquitetos.
3 Paulo Mendes da Rocha, interviewed by Ciro Miguel and José Paulo Gouvêa, August 2019.
4 Milton Braga, interview by the author, August 2019.
5 Ibid.
6 Ibid.
7 Ibid.
8 “Vitro Architectural Glass Formally Introduces Acuity Low-Iron Glass,” Vitro Architectural Glass, September 10, 2018, https://www.vitroglazings.com/about/news/vitro-architectural-glass-formally-introduces-acuity-low-iron-glass/.2
9 “Global Ultra Clear Glass Market 2019 to 2023,” *ReportsWeb*, June 2019, https://www.reportsweb.com/reports/global-ultra-clear-glass-market-2019-to-2023.
10 Ibid.
11 “Starphire® Technical Product Data,” Vitro Architectural Glass, April 2020, https://www.vitroglazings.com/media/gpvmzllx/vitro-starphire-vitro-technical-pds.pdf.
12 “Guardian Clarity,” Guardian Glass Industries, 2016, https://guardian.assetbank-server.com/assetbank-guardian/assetfile/22807.pdf.
13 “Solarban® 60 Solar Control Low E Glass,” Vitro Architectural Glass, accessed September 21, 2019, https://www.vitroglazings.com/products/low-e-glass/solarban-60-glass/.

14 "Glass Price Calculator," Crystal Glass and Mirror Corporation, accessed September 21, 2019, https://www.crystalglassny.com/Store/Glass-Products-Info.

15 "Glass Manufacturing Is an Energy-Intensive Industry Mainly Fueled by Natural Gas," U.S. Energy Information Administration, August 21, 2013, https://www.eia.gov/todayinenergy/detail.php?id=12631.

16 In 2018, Unimin and Fairmount Santrol merged to create a new company called Covia.

17 "Select Sands Begins Shipping Industrial Sand; Resource Estimate Increases 91%," Seeking Alpha, May 10, 2016, https://seekingalpha.com/article/3973544-select-sands-begins-shipping-industrial-sand-resource-estimate-increases-91-percent.

18 Ibid.

19 Sally Younger, "Sand Rush: Fracking Boom Spurs Rush on Wisconsin Silica," *National Geographic*, July 4, 2013, https://www.nationalgeographic.com/news/energy/2013/07/130703-wisconsin-fracking-sand-rush/.

20 Environmental Protection Declaration, "Vitro Architectural Glass Flat Glass Products," Vitro Architectural Glass, July 25, 2017, https://www.vitroglazings.com/media/nf0nm25r/vitro-epd-flat-glass-products.pdf.

21 Ibid.

22 Clarisse Cunha Linke, interview by the author, July 2019.

23 Ibid.

24 Ibid.

25 Saldiva, interview, July 2019.

26 Ibid.

27 Nascimento, interview, August 2019.

28 Saldiva, interview, July 2019.
29 Linke, interview, July 2019.
30 Ibid.
31 Ibid.
32 Colin Rowe and Robert Slutzky, "Transparency: Literal and Phenomenal," in *The Mathematics of the Ideal Villa and Other Essays* (Cambridge, MA: MIT Press, 2009), 116.

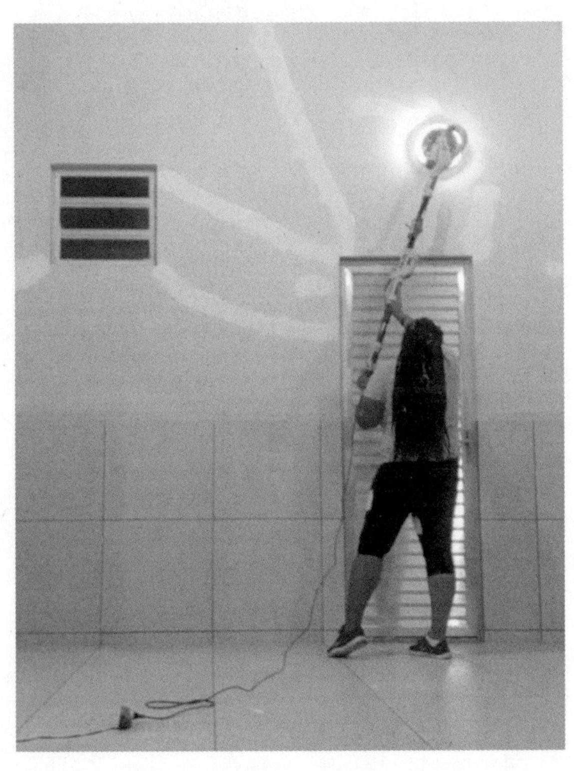

Concreto Rosa, drywall sanding

Repairing Objects and Built Environments

Geisa Garibaldi (Concreto Rosa)

My interest in civil construction started with activities I had dedicated myself to as a child, following the example of my mother. My mother was an active figure who did things at home. At the end of each year, for example, we would get together as a family to paint the house, an activity she would coordinate. I must have been about eight or nine years old when I first took part in this sacred ritual. When I was even younger I witnessed my mother build our own house. We lived in Baixada Fluminense, a very poor territory deprived of infrastructure. My mother was able to buy a piece of land, and from there she created the house, which then gradually changed over the years. When I was little, about four years old, the house was made of wood; when I was about eight or ten years old, it became a brick house roofed with Eternit; when I was fourteen years old, the house took its final shape, which is the house that my mother lives in today: a concrete-slab house. In other words, we gradually grew both financially and structurally. I believe my interest in civil construction came from this experience. I was the youngest daughter, and my brothers were already married with children when I was born. They moved onto the same plot, but in different houses.

My mother built the first wooden house herself. The second one, the brick house, was a collective effort. Although she dug the foundations on her own, at some point she needed to hire a construction worker to help with both the calculations and the structure. My mother had everything drawn in her head, which makes me think about her intuitive capacity to understand a field she never studied. Since the house was on rather muddy soil, about ten truckloads of red earth were brought in to build on. Everyone ended up participating in this gradual process, a collective endeavor where each of us got our hands dirty by aggregating concrete into the soil to structure it better.

Concrete's Political Economy and Gendered Significance

When I was young, I had the opportunity to collaborate in the construction of a concrete slab for the house of a couple who had just gotten married and did not have much money. It was a chance for me to earn a significant amount of money. Among the others on the construction site, mostly men, I participated by filling and lifting buckets, and helped to manage the operations as best I could. It was, however, an isolated experience. The journey from slab building to professional training course lasted almost a decade—meanwhile, I worked in an office, sitting at a desk. However, I always identified more with the proactive way of working with things—picking things up, making them, moving them up and down, getting my hands dirty—activities that are often seen as being "masculine." I do not know how to do my nails, I do not know how to do things delicately; I am a rougher woman.

During this period, it was on occasions like renting a property that I could accomplish things, although in an amateurish way: I asked my landlord if I could plaster the walls to get a discount on rent. After the experience with my family, civil-construction work returned to my life as a kind of barter system. But at the same time it was accompanied by a process of self-knowledge—of the way I see myself in the world—which ended up leading me to militant activism. What paved the way for me to seek a career in civil construction was that I started seeing it as one of the few areas in which women could receive the same remuneration as men.

The idea of founding Concreto Rosa came from a training course I had the chance to attend called "Projeto Mão na Massa" (Project Hands-On). This pioneering workshop was the idea of the civil engineer Deise Gravina, who realized that civil construction could be a way to professionalize women, especially low-income women who are in vulnerable conditions. It saw women's inclusion in the job market as a form of emancipation, gaining autonomy through their training to work as electricians, construction workers, carpenters, and painters. Throughout the course, I became more secure in relation to the profession, and I decided I would work with women for women. It would also be a way for me to develop my work as a form of activism, because there came a time when I could no longer participate in protests since I had to work. Thus I thought: "I will get the tools in order to fight not only for survival but also for my rights."

Before completing the course, I started to collaborate with some activist friends. They used to say to me, "I need help, but I do not want to have a man at home!" There were many women who refused to have men come into their home, not only because some were lesbians but because they were tired of the frequent dialogues with male service providers who are

Concreto Rosa, roof fixture

often sexist, violent, and do not take women's demands seriously. They did not feel safe opening their doors to these strangers, ultimately because they had had awful experiences in the past. My intention was to create a construction company staffed and run by women, since it was something that did not exist. However, in terms of a model for structuring this new business, I had no reference other than my mother's entrepreneurship.

We considered many names before coming up with Concreto Rosa. Initially we thought of using my last name plus the term "Renovations," which is common in Brazil: Fernando Renovations, João Renovations—and therefore Garibaldi Renovations. Alternative ideas were Yellow Hammer or Lilac Pliers. After a lot of speculation, and wanting to promote an idea of success, we concluded that it should be something related to a material we highly esteem: concrete. In Baixada Fluminense, where I grew up, to have a concrete house means to win in life, to say, "We made it." This is because concrete is expensive and more durable when compared to other construction materials such as brick. We finally came up with the name Concreto Rosa, thinking that concrete does not have to be gray—the gray color would be displaced as a feature often associated with something heavy and masculine. The idea was to give concrete another look. Concrete can be any color, a premise that certainly has a relationship with the LGBTQI+ movement. Concrete can be pink, lilac, blue, it can be "for boys" or "for girls." In our logo, the word "Concreto" is written in pink, "Rosa" is written in gray.

In Baixada, as well as in several regions of Brazil, houses are built incrementally, so the living room, kitchen, and bedroom all have different floor coverings. Since lack of funds is rather common, the construction of a house becomes an almost endless task—often a lifetime endeavor and struggle. This is the reality for many. It often starts with a little shack, followed by a slightly better construction covered with tile. The asbestos roof tile is celebrated like a birthday.[1] And when the concrete slab is poured, there is a great celebration of collective achievement. Nowadays there are prefabricated slabs, but back in the day pouring a slab was an occasion to bring everyone together, especially because many hands were needed. From my own experience and where I come from, I see concrete as a means to say, "This is my house, and my house was erected the way I want it." Nobody wants to live in a shack roofed with tile that heats up too much. A concrete slab means a minimum of comfort and quality of life. Concrete incarnates this freedom.

Means of Production and Professional Emancipation

Access to the means of production is what makes professional and entrepreneurial work on the construction site possible. Among the women who attended Projeto Mão na Massa with me, very few pursued careers in the civil-construction industry. It is not easy to enter and maintain oneself financially in this field. Even with the professional diploma in hand, it demands much sacrifice. The sacrifice has less to do with the heaviness of the work on the construction site than with the necessary investment in the equipment. And to invest in the means of production you must have a commission, and frequently to get a commission you must prove you have already done something. For this reason, many women tend to give up. I started with a tool kit that we obtained for free at the end of Projeto Mão na Massa, which symbolically became Concreto Rosa's first equipment—at home I had a Phillips screwdriver, but I did not even have a hammer! Little by little I obtained more commissions and was able to acquire new tools—first, a bad-quality drill, one of those that can only drill into walls at home. When I bought a professional Bosch drill, it was equivalent to the evolution from shack to concrete home. Every new step in this process would take me to the hardware store!

Yet the challenge is not only material. Within this predominantly male sector, the construction site constitutes a hostile environment for women. Not every woman feels at ease, because she knows she will be harassed, even if she wears a uniform. It is part of the construction culture! Furthermore, entrepreneurship also comes up against the lack of investment in female participation. It is difficult to find investors who are interested in putting together a construction site that employs women. This demands a certain level of organization and even the installation of differentiated infrastructure, such as cleaner bathrooms. The more you save, the better for investors. Concreto Rosa must therefore be self-sufficient in this sense, as an interdisciplinary contractor led by women, above all by Black women. Concreto Rosa brings together women professionals with various backgrounds—architects, urban planners, engineers, quarry workers, electricians—who in most cases do not even have the money to take public transportation. We have only recently been able to gain visibility through our own work, both inside and outside the construction site, relying not only on the tools we have acquired job after job, but on our cell phones: making videos, recording, and feeding social networks—virtual and real—that we have gradually built.

Domesticity and Care

I must, however, admit that this whole story has the domestic sphere as a starting point: the early days at my mother's house. The house is, historically, treated as the woman's concern: the care of the family, animals, things. It is the sphere of protection of human life, where affective memory is woven. Departing from the homely environment, a person can build his or her history. And a house, in Brazil, is something that is more and more difficult to achieve. A homeless man can sleep in a public square anywhere—his probability of being raped is minimal. This is not the case for a homeless woman. It is important to think of the house as a protection against violence. Concreto Rosa's action is also positioned in this sense: as a service focused on the integrity of women inside their home. Unfortunately, domestic violence can be exercised both within the family structure and by those who provide installation, repair, transportation, and moving services.

One of the cases that we addressed in our participation in the 12th International Architecture Biennale of São Paulo, the story of Dona Hellen from Bosque das Caboclas, a community located in Rio de Janeiro, remains a crucial reference point for me to speak about the construction of one's own house and home.[2] In 1992, Dona Hellen arrived at what was then an extremely inhospitable area, a veritable "no man's land." Most of the women there, all Black women, built practically the entire community on their own, thus contributing to the construction of the history of Campo Grande, a neighborhood in the western zone of the city. While they cleared the site's forest with their own hands, the men cooked. It was a question not only of strength but above all of disposition.

Women have this power. A precept associated with African deities, with the orishas, such as Oxum, goes: whatever does not have the hand of a woman cannot work. Unfortunately, we live in a society that does not partake of this premise, but we are moving forward. Racism is a way to undermine not only from the

Concreto Rosa, finished renovation

physical point of view—the annihilating of a body—but also from an emotional standpoint. I believe that today we are perhaps breaking more barriers because of these connections that associate the conquests of daily life with the sphere of work, from home to the urban space, and the planet as a whole.

Other Stories and Experiences

A great advancement, in this sense, concerns taking the reins of our own narratives: domestic urban and rural stories that start to be told by us Black women. This is a necessary advancement: to be able to tell our own story without the mediation of codes that are proper to European whiteness. When we talk about the Black population, we are mainly talking about an open code. Our code is more accessible and easier to read, linked to a true survival mechanism. Those who think about our territories, who can see them from a top-down, bird's-eye perspective, are different from the people who come from Baixada Fluminense, from the daily rush of life.

Cities need to be built considering our point of view. Concreto Rosa focuses on this dimension: of the micro-narratives related to the most intimate scale of human experience. It does so because it operates first and foremost in a sector in which other professionals of civil construction refuse to participate. Many do not want to respond to requests such as "I have a problem with my electrical resistance," or "I need to change a chandelier." The vast majority only want to provide a service that includes, for example, the demolition of a wall, for which they can charge a more significant fee. Concreto Rosa does not differentiate between the repair of a small problem like a leaky sink and the design, planning, and execution of a complete apartment renovation.

The most common services that we provide are day-to-day repairs, followed by painting and maintenance work. These repairs include electrical and hydraulic services, and sometimes an adjustment here or there, the installation of a mirror, a cabinet that must be fixed or merely mounted. "No water comes out of my toilet's discharge," "There are shortages of water in my house and my water tank no longer works," or "I have a problem with the fuse of my electric shower." We often share with these women a sort of care of the meaning of objects, environments, and interiors—lamps, mirrors, sinks, beds, bedrooms, bathrooms—however old some of them may be. Because they also tell stories. Many among those who request Concreto Rosa's services believe that they cannot have access to architectural design. But it is from these small repairs that we end up sealing a relationship of mutual trust, and from there we start to develop bigger works. Both sides gain access to architecture, to a new brand of construction, and, ultimately, to concrete!

Mabi Elu, a civil engineer, became one of Concreto Rosa's collaborators when she realized that she "was not the only one to find difficulties in exploring [her] powers in environments where [she] constantly suffers gender and racial prejudice, spaces that tend to be oppressive."[3] The architect and urban planner Emmily Leandro felt honored to join Concreto Rosa soon after she arrived in Rio de Janeiro, having been able to "get in touch with black women who are so engaged, doers, and inspirational in the area of civil construction."[4] As she recognizes, "Although I did my degree in architecture and urbanism in a class mostly populated by female students, when I started working in the field I did not have many partnerships with women in related areas, such as builders, painters, hydraulic specialists, and engineers." Still, according to Leandro, the relationships that were established and developed

Concreto Rosa, collective construction with women
at Bosque das Caboclas in Rio de Janeiro,
part of the project Mulheres em Ação (Women in Action)

through several projects resulted in a form of interaction that breaks from the professional mainstream. The relationships endorsed by Concreto Rosa foster a less hierarchical and more horizontal mode of interaction among women. For Elu, "This way of operating allows for more exchange and less imposition."

The almost affective bond that Concreto Rosa has established among women since the first works, as insignificant as it may seem, is what has allowed us to constitute real networks of solidarity. As Leandro states, "From our work it is possible to think of new forms of imagination of the daily life of civil construction, considering also the women who are building their own space in this field." In addition to the networks we have established with women to whom we provide varied services, we have joined forces with other professionals from the construction industry in Brazil.[5] We share with them, via WhatsApp, not only works but also knowledge and experiences—for instance, "Who knows how to remove this kind of screw?" Thanks to these networks, Concreto Rosa has become a living organism that moves throughout the city, and from time to time gathers in a coworking space. We have been contacted, for example, by a woman painter recently certified by Projeto Mão na Massa who was looking for a job, but also by engineers, and even by a man who sent us his resume. Today, as we have become more mature and confident both professionally and emotionally, we recognize that it is important to work together with men, that we need them as allies. We do not mean to say that men do not deserve to work, rather we are saying that women continue to earn less, that they have more responsibilities and fewer opportunities, especially Black women. It is the other who excludes. This is a lesson I brought from the comfort of my home: construction is a process that aggregates and exalts those who participate in it. It is a collective endeavor.

This essay is a transcription of an interview conducted by Vanessa Grossman, Charlotte Malterre-Barthes, and Ciro Miguel; it was edited by Vanessa Grossman and translated from the Portuguese by Vanessa Grossman with Ciro Miguel. All photographs are by Geisa Garibaldi.

1 It was only in 2017 that Brazil's Supreme Federal Court decided to ban the use of chrysotile asbestos, which was used in the manufacture of roofing sheets and water tanks.
2 The project Mulheres em Ação (Women in Action) was an initiative of the Coletiva Popular de Mulheres da Zona Oeste do Rio de Janeiro (Popular Collective of Women of the West Zone of Rio de Janeiro), an experience involving architecture and the emancipation of women in Bosque das Caboclas. In 2008, the Coletiva Popular searched for women professionals who could help them improve their houses, but it was only in 2019 that the project obtained funding. For one year women worked together with the Coletiva Popular, thinking and executing interventions in three houses: Dona Hellen's, Mara Rubia's, and Dona Isabel's. Several services were provided, such as installing gutters to collect rainwater, backyard landfill, and a garden to absorb rainwater. Concreto Rosa participated in the roof woodwork, which was one of the everyday stories presented as part of the project *Casa* at the 12th International Architecture Biennale of São Paulo, developed in collaboration with Concreto Rosa members Geisa Garibaldi, Mabi Elu, and Emmily Leandro. Among the objects exhibited was a roof tile

used in the renovation of Bosque das Caboclas, accompanied by an audio recording of Dona Hellen.

3 Mabi Elu, email to Geisa Garibaldi, June 23, 2020. Subsequent quotations by Elu are from this source.

4 Emmily Leandro, email to Geisa Garibaldi, June 23, 2020. Subsequent quotations by Leandro are from this source.

5 See Giovanna Maradei, "De mulheres para mulheres: Elas fazem reparos e reformas na sua casa!," *Casa Vogue*, January 16, 2019, https://casavogue.globo.com/Interiores/Ambientes/noticia/2019/01/de-mulheres-para-mulheres-elas-fazem-reparos-e-reformas-na-sua-casa.html.

Maintenance tools, Faculty of Architecture,
University of São Paulo, Brazil, 2019

Maintenance as a Political Act

Charlotte Malterre-Barthes

"It is still raining in our garage," wrote a distressed Madame Savoye to Le Corbusier in June 1930. Five years later, she reiterated: "It is raining in the hall, it's raining on the ramp and the wall of the garage is absolutely soaked. […] It's still raining in my bathroom, which floods in bad weather, as the water comes in through the skylight."[1] Leaks in Mies van der Rohe's and Frank Lloyd Wright's designs have become mythical.[2] To Richard Lloyd Jones, calling to complain about water dripping into his guest's soup, Wright answered, "The lady should move her chair."[3] After watching the documentary by Ila Bêka and Louise Lemoine that follows the painstaking journey of the housekeeper in his famously intricate Bordeaux house, Rem Koolhaas commented that he is irritated by the lack of creativity the cleaner shows, as she uses a "generic technique of cleaning [for] something so exceptional" as his designs.[4] Architects brush away issues they perceive as banal and domestic, seeing them as beyond their purview: users shall adapt to design and not the other way round; the maintenance of a building does not pertain to the discipline.

In the arts, care has been a central topic for decades, but it is only recently that architectural production and research have started to assimilate the indispensable nature of upkeep. To examine architectural designs through the lens of daily maintenance and the actions of the social and cultural identities of individuals within the space is to raise the question of for whom and by whom bodies, buildings, and infrastructure are maintained, at what cost, and through which means, resources, and mechanisms. Daily rituals of maintenance, either manual or automated, have emerged in full force against the backdrop of the health crisis of 2020. Bore by the bodies of people considered "unskilled," from housewives to cleaning staff, unjust labor divisions persist—the racist, classist, and sexist nature of domestic and maintenance work. Forcing the reevaluation of our daily sustenance systems and the tasks that support the infrastructure of our lives, everyday maintenance points toward the sociopolitical responsibility of architecture and planning disciplines in regard to care, repair, and decay.

First There Was Maintenance Art

A handshake with every single worker of New York City's Department of Sanitation—some 8,000 employees. This was Mierle Laderman Ukeles's first act, in 1979, as the department's unlikely, and unpaid, artist in residence. Ukeles is largely credited as the founder of "maintenance art," a term she coined in 1969 in a manifesto/proposal for the exhibition *Care*, conceptually linking maintenance to reproduction work, caring for humans, spaces, and the environment by placing everyday upkeep on the political terrain, raising questions of waste, labor, and gender.[5] Eco-feminism avant la lettre, Ukeles's view of the recurring, constant, eternal aspect of domestic care as a critical art form broke ground for further environmental and critical practices. Proof of this is the vivid updating of maintenance art as it expands to address racial injustice. In 2019, artist Sonya Clark performed a cleaning act by scrubbing the floor with a towel printed with the Confederate battle flag to reveal the sentence "We hold these truths to be self-evident."[6] Down on her knees, a woman of color wiping away allegorical historical dust, Clark tackles the ongoing racial and gendered aspect of domestic work that maintains spaces and bodies—one grounded in oppression. As philosopher Françoise Vergès has put it, referring to unpaid domestic work and the precarious jobs that guarantee clean offices, factories, cafeterias, schools, hospitals, and entire cities, "Without the women who wash it, the planet would stop turning."[7]

Leaks, Dirt, Feminism

Echoing the Villa Savoye's *dégâts des eaux*, architect and theorist Katherine Shonfield's essay "Why Does Your Flat Leak?" discusses leaks as construction mistakes, mastic performances, and structural honesty.[8] Spatial care as a concern of architectural design is brought forth by Shonfield by referring to an installation by the feminist practice Muf Architects entitled *Purity and Tolerance*, an allegorical work that compares the leakage of sanitary pads to that of buildings, in particular system-built paneled buildings. Weaving threads between body maintenance, hygiene, and building construction within the dichotomy of cleanliness and dirt, Shonfield and Muf Architects situate work on architecture and maintenance within an established strand of feminist theory: housework and care.

Yet if these topics have been consistently addressed in critical theory throughout the past decades—for instance, with sociologist Laura J. Miller's argument that domesticity within modernism functions as a tool to control female bodies[9]—this is less the case in the field of architectural design. Indicative of a possible recent resurgence, architect Hilary Sample's book *Maintenance Architecture* frames the myriad ways that building maintenance aligns with environmental performance, and advocates for recentering these topics at the core of design and architectural responsibility.[10] Stepping away from a critical understanding of spatial care and dissociating maintenance from "cleaning," this approach is slammed by feminist scholar Catherina Gabrielsson, who builds instead upon Nancy Fraser's feminist critique of capitalism to posit the double contradiction that exists between architecture and care as well as between capitalism and care.[11] The invisibility and lack of recognition of housework and social reproduction, while necessary to capitalism and wage labor, carry an economic perspective that is absent altogether from Sample's argumentation.

Others have tackled the relationship between architecture and care work in radical ways. In *Dirty Theory: Troubling Architecture*, Hélène Frichot embraces dirt as a conceptual tool in order to argue for building up "ethics of care and maintenance for our precarious environment-worlds."[12] In an online conversation in 2020, Frichot and Shannon Mattern discussed how the disciplines of architecture and planning have brushed away questions of repair, an omission pointed out in Mattern's remarkable article "Maintenance and Care."[13] From American Society of Civil Engineers reports on the bad condition of US infrastructure to citizens' self-initiated mending of potholes in their crumbling cities, the lack of repair emerges as political in comparison to consumerist ideologies and government shortcomings, as crucial to both the understanding and the functioning of modern cities and society—of technological culture at large.[14]

In 1996, the architecture practice Lacaton-Vassal won a design competition for the Place Leon Aucoc in Bordeaux. Rejected at first by municipal authorities whose expectations of a new gesture were crushed, their proposal was to simply intensify the maintenance protocols of the existing square. The project sent a statement of how potent spatial maintenance is, allowing for a pivoting of design toward a questioning of the archetypical assumption that architects must build anew by practicing methods of prolonging infrastructure. A similar shift materialized when Andrés Jaque literally brought to light the entire basement of Mies van der Rohe's Barcelona Pavilion, a celebration of the ordinary tasks required for the upkeep of the architectural icon. Jaque's 2013 installation gave dignity to the acts, objects, and spaces of maintenance, contrary to the invisibility of the efforts necessary to keep buildings from deteriorating.

Addressing the decay of the built environment, valuing the relentless labor necessary to fix failures and breakdowns, and resisting the urge to demolish and build anew—these are tasks a new generation of nontraditional collectives (Assemble, Rotor, and Mouraria 53, among others) have engaged with. Reclaiming what used to be common practice, they see preserving and recycling construction elements as key aspects in producing new works. Radically repositioned, these offices question construction and material economies, arguing for the added value to architectural projects supplied by reclaimed elements.

Can such logic be applied on a larger scale? Curators Angelika Fitz and Elke Krasny labeled architecture and urbanism that concerns the environment "critical care."[15] Large-scale interventions that have created resilient conditions for inhabitants, from flood protection to hospitable public space, show the path to perceiving the maintenance of nature and the built environment as a revolutionary practice. Advocating for a circular economy and repair in terms of materiality, attention to human and nonhuman living organisms, upkeep of clothes, goods, buildings, infrastructure, and the planet, spatial care is gaining traction.

The Political Nature of Maintenance

From the Morandi Bridge in Genoa to buildings in central Marseille, our everyday is populated with structures that collapse. To excuse their demise, politicians and officials are quick to blame the natural aging process or factors such as rain, squatting, or vandalism. Such aspects may play a role, but so does the lack of public funding for maintenance, a disengagement epitomized by budget cuts, privatization, outsourcing of cleaning and repair services, and a general contempt for upkeep efforts. An unspectacular task, maintenance work is contrary to new and grand projects deployed by populist politicians across the world, from Donald Trump's border wall to Recep Erdoğan's new Istanbul airport. The virile, one-off spectacular announcement of erecting a new massive piece of infrastructure is the antithesis of the gendered, banal, repetitive, eternal, selfless gestures of care provided to living organisms, homes, machines, objects, spaces, and infrastructures to guarantee their survival into another day.

In Western societies seeking to constantly create themselves anew, to maintain what exists is rather unpopular. Acts of preserving, nurturing, cleaning, and fixing are disrespected, perceived as dirty and irrelevant, and overwhelmingly performed by racialized and gendered low-paid laborers. If the caregiving labor of bodies and places came to light briefly in 2020, it is but high time to reevaluate its relevance. As calls grow

Structural maintenance, Marseille, 2019

Housekeeping, Haw Par Villa, Singapore, 2013

louder to decenter knowledge, deconstruct gender and racial injustice, and combat the climate emergency, the political potential of maintenance surfaces as both an act and a concept framed by the convergence of struggles—from ecofeminism to anti-capitalism to decolonizing movements. Maintenance, care, repair, reuse. It is no coincidence that Achille Mbembe, in a lecture from October 2020 on Africa's liberation from colonialism, called for "a vision of communities and organisms coexisting on this planet; sharing, repairing and preserving it, with Africa playing an exemplary role in working for global coexistence."[16] Maintenance, the discreet weapon of the world's underdogs under capitalism, is but a daily radical work of repeated gestures and activities, unstated yet essential. If considered a path to real sustainability, maintenance offers architecture the chance to completely reassess the value-generating chain of spatial production, pointing toward a possible way out from the crippling resource consumption generated by the construction industry. The evident yet radical act is thus not to build but to value and design spatial protocols of care and repair, allowing the world to function and appreciating those who make it work.

All photographs are by Charlotte Malterre-Barthes.

1 Cited in Jacques Sbriglio, *Le Corbusier: The Villa Savoye* (Basel: Birkhäuser, 1999), 147.
2 Cited in Nicole Sully, "Modern Architecture and Complaints about the Weather, or, 'Dear Monsieur Le Corbusier, It Is Still Raining in Our Garage…,'" *M/C Journal* 12, no. 4 (2009): 172.

3 Cited in Finis Farr, *Frank Lloyd Wright: A Biography* (New York: Charles Scribner's Sons, 1961), 272.

4 Hilary Sample, *Maintenance Architecture* (Cambridge, MA: MIT Press, 2016), 99.

5 Patricia C. Phillips et al., *Mierle Laderman Ukeles: Maintenance Art* (Munich: Prestel, 2016).

6 John Hurdle, "Rediscovering the Confederate Flag of Truce," *New York Times*, April 1, 2019, https://www.nytimes.com/2019/04/01/arts/design/confederate-flag-fabric-workshop-museum-sonya-clark.html.

7 Andrea D'Atri, "Françoise Vergès: 'Sans les femmes qui le nettoient, le monde arrêterait de tourner,'" *Révolution Permanente*, July 8, 2019, https://www.revolutionpermanente.fr/Francoise-Verges-sans-les-femmes-qui-le-nettoient-le-monde-arreterait-de-tourner.

8 See Katherine Shonfield, *Walls Have Feelings: Architecture, Film and the City* (London: Routledge, 2000), 32–52.

9 Laura J. Miller, "The Interiors of Frances Glessner Lee," in *Negotiating Domesticity: Spatial Productions of Gender in Modern Architecture*, ed. Hilde Heynen and Gulsum Baydar (London: Routledge, 2005), 197.

10 See Sample, *Maintenance Architecture*.

11 Catharina Gabrielsson, "The Critical Potential of Housework," in *Architecture and Feminisms: Ecologies, Economies, Technologies*, ed. Hélène Frichot, Catharina Gabrielsson, and Helen Runting (London: Routledge, 2018), 245–54.

12 Hélène Frichot, *Dirty Theory: Troubling Architecture* (Baunach: Spurbuchverlag, 2019), 180.

13 Shannon Mattern and Hélène Frichot, "Infrastructural Love in Times of COVID-19: Care, Repair,

and Maintenance," MSD at HOME, May 20, 2020, video, 1:08:31, https://msd.unimelb.edu.au/events/msd-at-home/msd-at-home-with-shannon-mattern; Shannon Mattern, "Maintenance and Care," *Places Journal* (November 2018), https://doi.org/10.22269/181120.

14 Stephen Graham and Nigel Thrift, "Out of Order: Understanding Repair and Maintenance," *Theory, Culture & Society* 24, no. 3 (May 2007): 1–25.

15 Angelika Fitz and Elke Krasny, eds., *Critical Care: Architecture and Urbanism for a Broken Planet* (Vienna: Architekturzentrum Wien, 2019).

16 Achille Mbembe, in conversation with Theory from the Margins, October 24, 2020, video, 1:44:09, https://youtu.be/sWHYQ6CqP20.

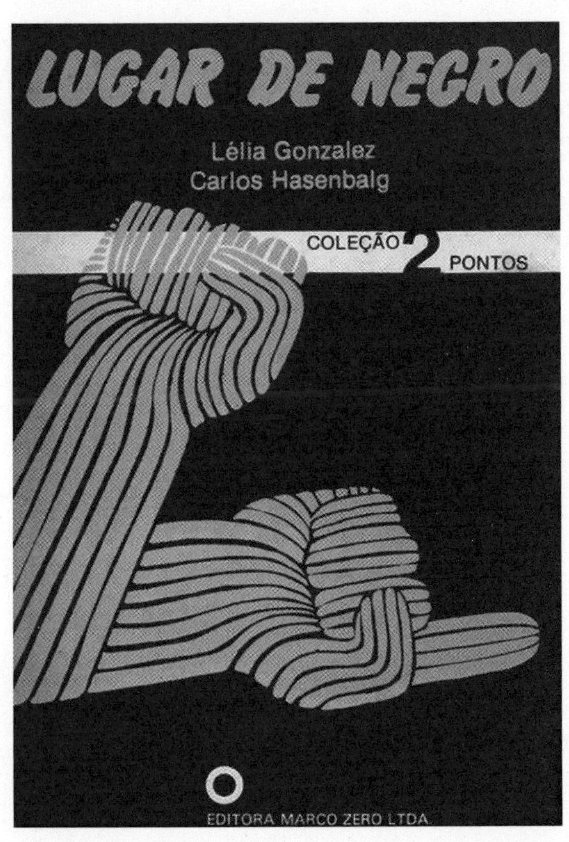

Cover of Lélia Gonzalez and Carlos Hasenbalg, *Lugar de negro*, 1982

Paths of Intersectionality in the Work of Lélia Gonzalez

Djamila Ribeiro

> The risk we take here is that of the act of speaking, with all its implications. It is exactly because we have been spoken to, infantilized (*infas* are those who do not have their own speech, the child who speaks of herself/himself in the third person, because she/he is spoken to by adults), that in this work we assume our own speech. That is, the trash here will speak, and in good faith.
>
> —Lélia Gonzalez[1]

A few years ago I was at the Guarulhos International Airport in São Paulo, waiting for my flight to Frankfurt, where I was going to give a lecture at a conference at the Cornelia Goethe Center for Women's and Gender Studies, an interdisciplinary research institute at the

Goethe-University, held within the framework of its Angela Davis Guest Professorship for International Gender and Diversity Studies. Nobody at the airport knew that—I was just a Black woman in a place where Black women are a dissonant presence. My Black female body sitting quietly at the boarding gate caused such discomfort that a white woman tapped me on the shoulder. I was wearing a headset to avoid any sort of interaction and looked over to see that she was waiting for me to acknowledge her. Taking a deep breath, I removed the headphones from my ears and made eye contact. "Hi," she said, "are you going on a trip?" I stared at her for a few moments thinking, No, I have been through check-in, through security, but I am here for a walk, I love to walk around airport departure lounges. Or even, and this is what she would have liked to hear, No, I am taking a break from my cleaning shift. Anyway, I said nothing of the sort—I usually adopt the "I'm not going to waste my time" tactic—so I answered, "Yes, of course." To which she said, "What are you going to do there? Are you going there to dance?" I replied, "No, why? Are you going there to dance?" Offended, she dropped the conversation.

Another time, I was in Berlin to participate in a literature festival. As a Black feminist from the southern hemisphere, invitations from the North feel a bit weird, to say the least. At this fair, for instance, I was paid airfare to speak about the political situation in Brazil for ten minutes and leave the next day—that is, a transatlantic trip to speak about Brazil on a panel with three white men. For ten minutes! Of these three, only one was Brazilian, a dear writer friend who, unlike me, was scheduled to talk about his work at other events at the fair. I accepted the invitation because it would give me a chance to adjust to the new time zone before I went on to Milan for another work engagement.

The moderator at the panel introduced each participant before they spoke. I was last in line. Each man presented his thoughts for much longer than the agreed time limit, speaking as much as he wanted, with the exception of my friend, perhaps because he is Brazilian and knows that, although the session's theme was the country in which we live, our vision was not "cocky" enough. After an hour, when my turn came, the mediator had "forgotten" my credentials. He did not know my first name, surname, or profession. To him, I was just a woman out on a walk, or, as my associate at the airport in Brazil said, there to dance. Well, my mother, Mrs. Erani Ribeiro dos Santos, taught me not to take things lying down. I took the floor and spent a good part of my speaking time introducing myself and talking about the transformative work I have done in Brazilian publishing, coordinating a collection on critical racial issues that has sold more than 300,000 copies, a historic achievement. I said that I was the most widely read nonfiction author in Brazil, not just the most widely read Black woman author; in fact, I am not infrequently the only Brazilian among the ten best-selling authors in the country. The Black Brazilian anthropologist and human-rights defender Lélia Gonzalez once said, "Black women must have a name and a surname, otherwise racism will give her any name it wants."

In this essay I will address the cultural-political category *Amefrican* (American African), which inscribes my body in everyday spaces that are not considered "natural" for someone like me. To understand what it is to be a woman outside her natural place, I will start with the aforementioned Brazilian thinker, who will guide my reflections. The overlooked work of Lélia Gonzalez (1935–1994) is at the center of my academic teaching. Gonzalez anticipated many debates in Black feminism even though she is not part of bibliographies on the theme, owing to Brazil's geopolitical position in the Southern Hemisphere. Gonzalez wrote about the "expected place"; paraphrasing Aristotle's reflections on physics in her 1982 work *Lugar de negro* (The place of the black person), Gonzalez interprets the "expected place" of the Black man or woman in public space in Brazil as follows:

> From colonial times to the present day, we can see a clear separation in the physical space occupied by the dominators and the dominated. The natural place for the dominant white group consists of large, spacious houses located in the most beautiful corners of the city or countryside and duly protected by different types of policing: from the old slave overseers, bounty hunters, henchmen, etc., to the formally constituted police. From the *casagrande* [or "big house," referring to a slave owner's residence] and the *sobrado* [colonial-era two-story house] to today's beautiful buildings and residences, the criterion has always been the same. The natural place of the Black person is, of course, the opposite: from the slaves' quarters to slums, tenements, basements, squatter settlements, swamps, and today's housing estates (whose models are the ghettos of developed countries), the criterion has been symmetrically the same: racial and spatial division.[2]

A Black woman in the waiting area of an international boarding gate—that is, a Black Brazilian woman—or speaking at a book festival in Germany is not in her natural place, and produces a strangeness around her with undetermined consequences. In my case, being Brazilian, I am not only out of place as a Black woman but also out of the expected place of the Black Brazilian woman from the perspective of the Global North, meaning a Black woman as a "*mulatta* for export" who joyfully dances samba half-naked around a table of white and Black men to the sound of the *pandeiro*, a Brazilian tambourine. The mulatta is a fundamental part of Brazil's "racial democracy" that is portrayed abroad. Her natural place in accepting male advances may explain the absurd number of foreigners from the Global North that come to the country for sex tourism, often with teenagers.

Here I will briefly analyze the paths of intersectionality in the vast production of Lélia Gonzalez, who was a professor of sociology at the Pontifical Catholic University of Rio de Janeiro. The concept of intersectionality, developed by Black women activists for over a century, received greater attention when the American critic and theorist Kimberlé Crenshaw systematized it in a paper in 1989, five years before Gonzalez's death, to analyze how race, gender, and class intersect and generate different forms of oppression. According to Crenshaw: "Intersectionality is a conceptualization of the problem that seeks to capture the structural and dynamic consequences of the interaction between two or more axes of subordination. It specifically addresses the manner in which racism, patriarchy, class oppression, and other discriminatory systems create inequalities that structure the relative positions of women, races, ethnicities, classes, and others."[3]

In a 2019 article, the Black Brazilian feminist Carla Akotirene expressed the power of intersectionality in formulating public policies, since "it is through intersectionality that nation-states assumed the signatory commitment to create laws and public policies after the World Conference in Durban, South Africa, in 2001, to combat racism, racial discrimination, related violence, intolerance, and xenophobia."[4]

The author points out that after the conference, public policies were anchored by the administration of Brazil's then president Luiz Inácio da Silva, known as Lula, especially by the ministers Mathilde Ribeiro and Luiza Bairros:

> If today we are able to execute racial policy in Education, Health, Culture, Agrarian Development, we should refer to ministries such as SEPPIR (Special Secretary of Policies for the Promotion of Racial Equality) and the demographic racial redistribution of opportunities implemented by the Left anchored in the post-Durban actions. The specialists were instrumentalized by the intellectual production of Kimberlé Crenshaw, notably the "Background Paper for the Expert Meeting on the Gender-Related Aspects of Race Discrimination"(2002); they engaged in the antiracist, antisexist, nondenominational struggle and finally understood the form of laws and legal design of the way sectorial public policies are transversally effected.[5]

In a 2013 article, the political scientist and gender-studies scholar Cristiano Rodrigues explains that the production of race and gender categories has been present in Black Brazilian feminist thought that deals with the specificity of Black women, breaking with the universalization of womanhood. In this sense, theoreticians such as Luiza Bairros, Sueli Carneiro, Mathilde Ribeiro, Zélia Amador de Deus, and Edna Roland, among many others, tried to build the theoretical foundations of Black Brazilian feminism under inhospitable conditions, such as the structural oppression of the country's geopolitical positioning, which confined it to a permanent situation of colonial exploitation, allowing for limited access to material opportunities for development.

In Brazil, Black people were forbidden from receiving an education under the first constitution of 1824 and even after slavery was abolished in 1888. The last country in the West to abolish slavery, it also had no policy for inserting Black people into society. Black women were confined to domestic work, and those who managed to transcend this faced colonial obstacles to disseminating their ideas. Encountering much struggle and scarce opportunities, Black women began to organize politically in academia in 1980, the year in which Gonzalez presented her first and celebrated article, "Racismo e sexismo na sociedade brasileira." As Rodrigues explains: "In this article, Gonzalez is interested in thinking about how the articulation between sexism and racism functions as one of the symbolic operators of the way Black women are seen and treated in the country. For the author, racism and sexism engender violence against Black women and explain the fact that even middle-class Black women are victims of discrimination. In other words, one cannot understand the discrimination and oppression suffered by women only through gender and social class biases."[6]

Two years later, Gonzalez published "A mulher negra na sociedade brasileira,"[7] in which she situated the Black Brazilian woman as the target of racial, gender, and class oppression by white women. Rodrigues writes: "The author focuses her analysis on the fact that not paying attention to the racial issue demarcates the complicity of white women in the domination of Black women. Thus, by focusing only on the categories of gender and class, studies on Brazilian women contribute to the naturalization of racial inequalities. For Gonzalez, Black women are victims of a triple oppression: race, gender, and social class."[8]

The idea of theorizing from the intersection of oppressions and identities of oppressed social groups arose historically within Black feminism. Even if American abolitionist and women's-rights activist Sojourner Truth is not considered a feminist in the strict sense of the term, already in the nineteenth century, in her speech "Ain't I a Woman?," she criticized the universality of woman as a category. Corroborating the analysis of Rodrigues, Akotirene stresses Gonzalez's pioneering approach in her book *Interseccionalidade*, referring to studies by Gonzalez's biographers: "The biography of Lélia Gonzalez [...] by Alex Ratts and Flavia Rios uses the black feminist tone to present Oxum, the thinker's ruling orisha, nationality, gender, and class, moving the non-linear, non-objective, and non-neutral intellectual texture of intersectionality and revealing ancestral arrangements, especially in the 1980s. Then they publish 'A perspectiva interseccional de Lélia Gonzalez,' confirming the conceptual anticipation of intersectionality in the thinker 'who, as an academic activist, articulated racism, sexism and capitalist exploitation.'"[9]

However, the anticipations of and commentaries on intersectionality from the Global North are diffused by the epistemic privilege derived from the geopolitical privilege of nations that actualize the mechanisms of colonization in the South. The ideas developed by Black North American feminists are certainly important; they undoubtedly serve as both a foundation and a source. Even though they are located in the Global North they are not hegemonic, and they contribute decisively to a displacement and deepening of the Black feminist project. Yet, because they are in the Global North, these works gain more space and are more widely translated, and one runs the risk of thinking of Black feminisms only through their lens. While the importance of Black American feminism must be recognized, it is important to question the colonial politics of translation.

Translation policy as a mechanism to break with the erasure of vulnerable groups is a part of the editorial work being developed in Brazil. I am the director of the Sueli Carneiro imprint, named in honor of the great Black Brazilian feminist, which aims to publish critical racial studies by Black women and men for a national and international audience, especially through the Coleção Feminismos Plurais (Plural Feminisms Collection). In 2018, the imprint published a volume of Sueli Carneiro's collected writings, *Escritos de uma vida*; like the illustrious Brazilian novelist Conceição Evaristo, Carneiro had to wait until she was seventy to have her work available in Brazilian bookstores. Books published by the imprint have been translated into French, Spanish, and Italian, and book tours have allowed the authors to spread not only their own thinking but Black Brazilian thinking as a whole.

On a recent trip to Brazil, American political activist and philosopher Angela Davis asked why they want to listen to her in Brazil when the country has Lélia Gonzalez. The answer to this incisive question lies, on the one hand, in the geopolitical position of the Global South, and on the other, in the lack of sisterhood between Black women of the North and South. For people to want to listen to Davis, it was first necessary for her work to be translated and published in Brazil—that is, it required the initiative and effort of Black women in the country, including me. If a small number of people know about Lélia Gonzalez in the North, it is because her work hasn't been translated—the politics of academic citation also need to be questioned as a mechanism for maintaining epistemic privilege. So much has been produced about solidarity, and yet Black women in South America still wonder when this idea will be put into practice. Since it has not been, as was evident at the panel in Berlin where the moderator "forgot" my name, it is time for us to do it ourselves.

On the South American continent, Black feminists break not only with the universalism of white women but also with the epistemic matrices of domination derived from North American imperialism. To understand the paths of intersectionality in Gonzalez's work, it is important to refer to the points from where she started those paths. Coming to the end of this text, rather than looking at the branches and leaves, I will look at the roots. Where did Gonzalez's path begin? The first step is to analyze her identity inscribed in *Amefricanidade*, a fundamental step to break with "American" universalism. In Gonzalez's words:

> The terms Afro-American and African-American bring us to a first thought: that there are Blacks only in the United States and not in both continents. Furthermore, they point to the unconscious reproduction of the imperialist position of the United States, claiming to be "THE AMERICA." After all, what about the countries of South, Central, Insular, and North AMERICA? Why should we consider the Caribbean as something separate, if it was precisely there that the history of this AMERICA began? It is interesting to observe that someone who leaves Brazil, for example, says that he is going to "America." And that all of us, from any region of the continent, do the same, perpetuating the imperialism of the United States, calling its inhabitants "Americans." And what about us, what are we, Asians?
>
> The political and cultural implications of the category of *Amefricanidade* are indeed democratic, precisely because the term itself allows us to go beyond territorial, linguistic, and ideological

> limitations, opening up new perspectives for a deeper understanding of that part of the world where it manifests itself: AMERICA as a whole (South, Central, North, and Insular). Beyond its purely geographical character, the category of *Amefricanidade* incorporates a whole historical process of intense cultural dynamics [...]. Consequently, it leads us toward the construction of an entire ethnic identity.[10]

Following Lélia Gonzalez's path, one finds the questioning of a system of structural domination based on race, class, gender, and geopolitics that organizes the epistemologies of the Global South. It is a powerful analytical tool for the plurality of existences and knowledge, and for one's very insertion and resistance in everyday spaces and places of oppression that persist across international borders.

Translated from the Portuguese by Vanessa Grossman with Ciro Miguel

1 Lélia Gonzalez, "Racismo e sexismo na sociedade brasileira" [Racism and sexism in Brazilian society], in *Pensamento Feminista Brasileiro: Formação e contexto* (Rio de Janeiro: Bazar do Tempo, 2019), 239.
2 Lélia Gonzalez and Carlos Hasenbalg, *Lugar de negro* (Rio de Janeiro: Marco Zero, 1982), 15.
3 Kimberlé Crenshaw, "Documento para o encontro de especialistas em aspectos da discriminação racial relativos ao gênero," trans. Liane Schneider, *Revista de Estudos Feministas* 10, no. 1 (2002): 177.
4 Carla Akotirene, "Ferramenta anticolonial poderosa: Os 30 anos de interseccionalidade" [A powerful

anti-colonial tool: 30 years of intersectionality], *Carta Capital*, September 18, 2019, https://www.cartacapital.com.br/opiniao/ferramenta-anticolonial-poderosa-os-30-anos-de-interseccionalidade/.

5 Akotirene.

6 Cristiano Rodrigues, "Atualidade do conceito de interseccionalidade para a pesquisa e prática feminista no Brasil" [Current status of the concept of intersectionality for feminist research and practice in Brazil], *Seminário Internacional Fazendo Gênero*, no. 10 (2013): 3.

7 Lélia Gonzalez, "A mulher negra na sociedade brasileira" [The Black woman in Brazilian society], in *O lugar da mulher, estudos sobre a condição feminina na sociedade atual*, ed. Madel T. Luz (Rio de Janeiro: Graal, 1982), 89–106.

8 Rodrigues, "Atualidade do conceito de interseccionalidade," 4.

9 Carla Akotirene, *Interseccionalidade* (São Paulo: Jandaíra, Coleção Feminismos Plurais), 33.

10 Lélia Gonzalez, "A categoria político-cultural da Amefricanidade" [The political-cultural category of Amefricanidade], in *Pensamento Feminista: Conceitos fundamentais*, ed. Heloisa Buarque de Almeida (Rio de Janeiro: Bazar do Tempo, 2019), 348–49.

Acknowledgments

This book grew out of conversations that began between Zurich and Toronto in 2018, unfolded and took shape during *Todo dia/Everyday*, the 12th International Architecture Biennale of São Paulo (September–December 2019), and continued between Zurich and Delft. We are grateful to all of those who made these intellectual journeys possible. First and foremost, we would like to thank the contributors to this book: Beatriz Colomina and Mark Wigley, Caitlin DeSilvey, Geisa Garibaldi, Anna Heringer, Andrés Jaque, Guillermo López and Anna Puigjaner, Charlotte Malterre-Barthes, Markus Miessen, Mouraria 53, Djamila Ribeiro, Renzo Taddei, and Ilze and Heinrich Wolff. We would also like to thank the São Paulo Department of the Instituto de Arquitetos do Brasil (IABsp), Serviço Social do Comércio (Sesc), Centro Cultural São Paulo, and the cocurators, producers, designers, open-call jury, participants, and visitors of the biennale. Without the Graham Foundation for Advanced Studies in the Fine Arts the publication of this book would not have been possible. We thank the Graham for its essential support, in particular Sarah Herda, James Graham, and Carolyn Kelly. We also thank ETH Zurich's Department of Architecture for the material and intellectual support for this book, in particular Tom Avermaete, Brigitte Beck, Arno Brandlhuber, Irina Davidovici, Momoyo Kaijima, Zeljko Medved, Laurent Stalder, Alexandre Theriot, Philip Ursprung, and Jan De Vylder. We are grateful to Ilka and Andreas Ruby for believing in the project and contributing to it through fruitful exchanges. We are also thankful to Jean-Louis Cohen, Alexis Kalagas, Nelson Mota, and Ilka Ruby for their invaluable input and insight as careful readers of this book. Marc Angélil and Jean-Louis Cohen are not only mentors but major supporters of the grant applications that allowed this publication to come to life. We are particularly indebted to Leonard Streich and Something Fantastic for the creative exchanges, and to Lukas Burkhart and Elli Mosayebi for allowing us to use, on the book cover, the image of *Water,* the silky spatial intervention they produced for the 12th International Architecture Biennale of São Paulo. We thank Max Bach for his copyediting, suggestions, and input. We are grateful for the help and contributions of Silvia Gomes, Roberto González García, Emmily Leandro, Leslie Loretto, and Mabi Elu Santos. We thank our professors, colleagues and friends Lucia Allais, Pablo Alvarenga, Francesca Angiolillo, Amanda Antunes, Taneha Bacchin, Martina Baum, Thiago Benucci, Céline Bessire, Juliana Braga, Angelo Bucci, Martha Bucci, Wellington Cançado, Maurício Candeloro, Diego Ceresuela, Alexandre Delijaicov, Luana Demange, Guillermo Dürig, Facundo Fernandez, Felipe De Ferrari, Darío Graschinsky, Sarah Hayes, Dirk van den Heuvel, Karina Hüssner, Daniel Jabra, Anne Kockelkorn, Barend Koolhaas, Aura Luz Melis, Noelia Monteiro, Nelson Mota, Laure Nashed, Eduardo Nasser, Daniela Ortiz dos Santos, Spyros Papapetros, Francesco Perrotta-Bosch, Guilherme Pianca, Pedro Rivera, Javier Agustín Rojas, Marcos Rosa, Lola Sheppard, Leonid Slonimskiy, João Sodré, Davide Spina, Daniel Talesnik, Carol Tonetti, Sevgi Türkkan, Catherine Venart, Mariana Vilela, Markus Vogl, Enrique Walker, Mason White, Eleanor Willi, Matthias Winter, and Lydia Xynogala for their fruitful exchanges; João Guilherme Dal Fabbro for his essential assistance with the legal aspects related to the book's completion; and Márcio Grossman, Déborah Zaverucha Grossman, Thalita Grossman, Dorothéa Lola Pinkusfel Grossman, Eloísa Grossman, João Paulo Miguel, Cristina Miguel, Caio Miguel, and our extended families and other friends who helped us accomplish this project. We are deeply indebted to Sophie Piticco and Andreas Sakellaris for their patience in dealing with our ups and downs and for their positiveness and creative input. Noah and Elias Sakellaris have interfered productively and unproductively in the book's conception, and are certainly the main source of inspiration for their mother. This book is also the outcome of more than two decades of friendship, intellectual exchange, jokes, online messages, and life experience shared by us, its editors.

Contributors

Beatriz Colomina is an internationally renowned architectural historian and theorist who has written extensively on architecture, art, technology, sexuality, and media. She is founding director of the interdisciplinary Program in Media and Modernity at Princeton University and professor and director of graduate studies in the School of Architecture. Published in more than 25 languages, her books include: *Are We Human? Notes on an Archaeology of Design* (Lars Müller Publishers, 2016), *The Century of the Bed* (Verlag für moderne Kunst, 2015), *Das Andere/The Other: A Journal for the Introduction of Western Culture into Austria* (MAK Center for Art and Architecture, 2016), *Manifesto Architecture: The Ghost of Mies* (Sternberg Press, 2014), *Clip, Stamp, Fold: The Radical Architecture of Little Magazines, 196X–197X* (Actar Publishers, 2010), *Domesticity at War* (MIT Press, 2007), *Privacy and Publicity: Modern Architecture as Mass Media* (MIT Press, 1994), and *Sexuality and Space* (Princeton Architectural Press, 1992). She has curated a series of international exhibitions based on archival and oral-history research to communicate research to a wider audience with physical installations, digital platforms, and new forms of publication, including, most recently, the 3rd Istanbul Design Biennial (2016) on the theme *Are We Human? The Design of the Species*.

Caitlin DeSilvey is professor of cultural geography at the University of Exeter. Her research explores the cultural significance of material change and transformation, with a particular focus on heritage contexts. She has worked with artists, archaeologists, environmental scientists, and heritage practitioners on a range of interdisciplinary projects. Although much of her research is about how things (and places) fall apart, she is also interested in the practices of repair and maintenance that hold things together. She is author of *Curated Decay: Heritage beyond Saving* (University of Minnesota Press, 2017), coauthor of *Visible Mending: Everyday Repairs in the South West* (Uniformbooks, 2013), and coeditor of *Anticipatory History* (Uniformbooks, 2011).

Concreto Rosa is a Rio de Janeiro–based practice founded by Geisa Garibaldi. Its main objective is to grant the power of social participation to women, ensuring that they are aware of their rights, such as total equality among races and genders, in a predominantly male field. Concreto Rosa's collaborators are primarily Black women working as bricklayers, architects, or electrical, hydraulic, or civil engineers. Rather than considering those who commission their work as mere customers, they establish networks of solidarity that surpass the mercantile relations often in play between clients and service providers, cooperating professionals, or subjects and objects. Their work coordinates complex systems of making, design, transportation, maintenance, and care, while enduring the social, racial, gender, and even geographical biases that characterize Brazilian society.

Vanessa Grossman is assistant professor in the Faculty of Architecture and the Built Environment, Delft University of Technology. She is an architect, historian of modern and contemporary architecture, and curator whose research focuses on architecture's intersections with ideology, power, housing, and governance, with a special focus on global practices in Cold War–era Europe and Latin America. Grossman earned her doctoral degree in the history and theory of architecture from Princeton University. She is the author of, among other books and writings, *Le PCF a changé! Niemeyer et le siège du Parti communiste, 1966–1981* (Éditions B2, 2013) and *A arquitetura e o urbanismo revisitados pela Internacional Situacionista* (Annablume/FAPESP, 2006); coauthor of *Oscar Niemeyer en France: Un exil créatif* (Éditions du patrimoine, 2021); and coeditor of *AUA: Une architecture de l'engagement, 1960–1985* (Cité de l'architecture et du patrimoine / Dominique Carré Éditeur, 2015) and *Modernity, Promise or Menace? France, 101 buildings, 1914–2014* (Institut français / Dominique Carré Éditeur, 2014). She was cocurator of *Todo dia/Everyday*, the 12th International Architecture Biennale of São Paulo (2019) and *Une architecture de l'engagement: L'AUA, 1960–1985* (2015–16) at the Cité de l'architecture et du patrimoine in Paris, among other exhibitions.

Anna Heringer is an architect based in Germany and honorary professor of the UNESCO Chair of Earthen Architecture, Building Cultures, and Sustainable Development whose work focuses on the use of natural building materials. Since 1997 she has been actively involved in development cooperation in Bangladesh. Her diploma project, the METI school in Rudrapur, was realized in 2005 in collaboration with

Eike Roswag-Klinge and won the Aga Khan Award for Architecture in 2007. Over the years, Heringer has realized further projects in Asia, Africa, and Europe. Together with Martin Rauch she developed the method of clay storming, which she teaches at various universities worldwide. In 2013, she initiated the Laufen Manifesto with Andres Lepik and Hubert Klumpner, in which practitioners and academics from around the world contributed guidelines for a humane design culture.

Andrés Jaque / Office for Political Innovation (OFFPOLINN) is an international architectural practice based in New York and Madrid. Working at the intersection of design, research, and critical environmental practices, the office develops projects in different scales and media that intend to bring inclusivity into the built environment. In 2016, OFFPOLINN received the Frederick Kiesler Prize from the city of Vienna; the office has also been awarded the Silver Lion for Best Research Project at the 14th Venice Biennale and the Dionisio Hernández Gil Award. Jaque's numerous books and writings include *Superpowers of Scale* (Columbia University Press, 2020), *Mies y la gata Niebla* (Puente Editores, 2019), *Calculable* (Ediciones ARQ, 2016), and *PHANTOM: Mies as Rendered Society* (Fundació Mies van der Rohe, 2013).

MAIO is a Barcelona and New York–based architectural office that works on spatial systems that allow variation through time. Its projects embrace the ever-changing complexity of everyday life while providing a resilient, compromised, and clear architectural response. Founded in Barcelona in 2012, MAIO is run by Maria Charneco, Alfredo Lérida, Guillermo López, and Anna Puigjaner, who was a finalist of the Rolex Mentor & Protégé Initiative 2016 and was awarded the 2016 Wheelwright Prize from the Harvard Graduate School of Design. Their work has been published in magazines worldwide and exhibited at New York's Museum of Modern Art and Storefront for Art and Architecture, the Guggenheim Bilbao, and the Art Institute of Chicago.

Charlotte Malterre-Barthes is an architect, researcher, and assistant professor of urban design at the Harvard Graduate School of Design. Her teaching and research interests are related to urgent aspects of contemporary urbanization and how struggling communities can gain greater access to resources, the mainstream economy, better governance, and ecological/social justice. Malterre-Barthes earned her doctoral degree while directing the Master of Advanced Studies in Urban Design at ETH Zurich. She is coeditor of *Migrant Marseille: Architectures of Social Segregation and Urban Inclusivity* (Ruby Press, 2020) and *Housing Cairo: The ~~Informal~~ Response* (Ruby Press, 2016) and coauthor of *Some Haunted Spaces in Singapore* (Edition Patrick Frey, 2018). Malterre-Barthes is a founding member of the Parity Group and the Parity Front, activist networks dedicated to improving gender equality in architecture. She was cocurator of *Todo dia/Everyday*, the 12th International Architecture Biennale of São Paulo (2019).

Markus Miessen is an architect, researcher, and writer. He received his PhD from the Centre for Research Architecture / Forensic Architecture at Goldsmiths, London. His work revolves around questions of critical spatial practice, institution building, and spatial politics. Miessen has taught at AA (London), Städelschule (Frankfurt am Main), and USC (Los Angeles), and has been a Harvard fellow. His Berlin-based design practice, Studio Miessen, works closely with a number of artists, such as Hito Steyerl and Flaka Haliti, and is involved in the spatial reconceptualization of the Gropius Bau Berlin. Among other books and writings, he is the author of *Crossbenching* (Sternberg Press, 2016) and *The Nightmare of Participation* (Sternberg Press, 2010). Miessen is currently associate professor in urban regeneration at the University of Luxembourg.

Ciro Miguel is an architect, photographer, and doctoral fellow of the Institute for History and Theory of Architecture at ETH Zurich. His research focuses on the intersections between architecture, photography, and mass media. He holds a professional diploma from the University of São Paulo FAU USP and a master's degree from Columbia University GSAPP. At ETH Zurich, Ciro taught architectural design under Angelo Bucci (2013) and Marc Angélil (2014–19). As a practitioner, he was a partner of SPBR arquitetos for many years, and still collaborates with the office. His work has been exhibited at biennials in Venice and São Paulo and in museums such as Architekturmuseum der TUM in the Pinakothek der Moderne, S AM Basel, Center for Architecture New York, Pavillon de l'Arsenal, São Paulo Museum of Modern Art, and the Het Nieuwe Instituut. He was cocurator of *Todo dia/Everyday*, the 12th International Architecture Biennale of São Paulo (2019).

Mouraria 53 is an interdisciplinary collective that emerged from the process of renovating a ruin in the historic center of Salvador in northeastern Brazil. Their work involves construction and design as well as exhibitions, a psychology clinic, and studies in photojournalism. The collective is conceived as an attempt to engage existing networks of the city within a process of architecture, including the disposal of construction residue and the emerging music scene. Both the house and its collective change members and programs over the years.

Djamila Ribeiro holds a master's degree in political philosophy from the Federal University of São Paulo and is coordinator of the Feminismos Plurais book series. She is the author of *Lugar de fala* (Pólen Livros, 2019), *Pequeno manual antirracista* (Companhia das Letras, 2019), and *Quem tem medo do feminismo negro?* (Companhia das Letras, 2018), and is a columnist for the newspaper *Folha de São Paulo*. In 2019 the BBC named Ribeiro one of the 100 most influential women in the world, and in 2020 she won the Jabuti Award in the category of human sciences.

Something Fantastic was founded in 2010 by Elena Schütz, Julian Schubert, and Leonard Streich after their studies in architecture at the University of the Arts Berlin and ETH Zurich, based on the conviction that architecture is related to everything, and the resulting social, ecological, and political responsibility should lead to a different kind of practice. The oeuvre of the non-disciplinary office includes research and teaching in addition to the conception and design of books, exhibitions, furniture, buildings, and urban planning. The office's work has been exhibited at biennials in Venice, São Paulo, and Shenzhen, as well as in museums such as BOZAR Brussels, MAR Rio de Janeiro, and MoMA New York. Since 2019, after teaching at the MAS Urban Design at ETH Zurich, the partners have been heading the Space Department at the Gerrit Rietveld Academie in Amsterdam. Their current visiting professorship at the Peter Behrens School of Architecture in Düsseldorf is entitled "All-Inclusive Urbanism."

Renzo Taddei teaches anthropology and science and technology studies at the Federal University of São Paulo. He earned his doctoral degree in anthropology from Columbia University. Taddei has served as visiting scholar at Yale University, Duke University, and the University of the Republic in Montevideo, Uruguay. He is a research associate at the Center for Research on Environmental Decisions at Columbia University. Taddei's writings deal with the variety of ways in which humans in South America interact with the atmosphere, climate and climate change, environmental conflicts, and traditional environmental knowledge.

Mark Wigley is professor and dean emeritus at the Columbia Graduate School of Architecture, Planning and Preservation, where he served as dean from 2004 to 2014. He has written extensively on the theory and practice of architecture, and is the author of *Constant's New Babylon: The Hyper-Architecture of Desire* (Witte de With, 1998); *White Walls, Designer Dresses: The Fashioning of Modern Architecture* (MIT Press, 1995); and *The Architecture of Deconstruction: Derrida's Haunt* (MIT Press, 1993). He coedited *The Activist Drawing: Retracing Situationalist Architectures from Constant's New Babylon to Beyond* (MIT Press, 2001). In 2005 he cofounded *Volume* magazine with Rem Koolhaas and Ole Bouman as a collaborative project between Archis (Amsterdam), AMO (Rotterdam), and C-Lab (Columbia University). Wigley curated *Deconstructivist Architecture* (1988) at the Museum of Modern Art, New York, as well as other exhibitions at the Drawing Center, New York; Canadian Centre for Architecture, Montreal; and Witte de With, Rotterdam.

Wolff Architects is a Cape Town–based design studio concerned with developing an architectural practice of consequence through the mediums of design, advocacy, research, and documentation. Led by Ilze and Heinrich Wolff, the team includes a group of highly skilled, committed, and engaged architects, creative practitioners, and administrators. Heinrich is an architect and project manager with over twenty years of experience who has held several academic appointments. Ilze is a partner at Wolff Architects and cofounder and director of the Open House Architecture in 2007, a transdisciplinary research practice.

Image Credits

© Ciro Miguel: cover, 108-22
© Ester Carro: 10, 12
© Erica Overmeer: 22
© Pedro Kok: 26
© Thiago Benucci: 27
© Ana Cuba: 34, 36, 39, 40, 43, 44, 47
© Dave Southwood: 50, 59
© *pumflet: art, architecture and stuff*: 55
© Wolff Architects: 52, 57, 60
© Peter Bauerndick: 62
© Norbert Rau: 65
© Benjamin Stähli: 68, 73
© Stefano Mori: 71
© Alan dos Anjos: 76, 87
© Pedro Alban: 80, 85
© Fernando Gomes: 84, 88, 90
© Zak Group: 94
© JongOh Kim: 98, 100
© Pablo Ferao: 101
© Naho Kubota: 104
© The Miriam and Ira D. Wallach Division of Art, Prints and Photographs, Print Collection, New York Public Library, New York Public Library Digital Collections: 124, 128, 133, 136, 139
© Russell Johnston and Caitlin DeSilvey: 142, 148, 150, 153
© Museum of Cornish Life, Helston, Cornwall: 145
© Office for Political Innovation: 156, 159, 160, 163, 166, 169, 170
© Geisa Garibaldi: 176, 180, 185, 188
© Charlotte Malterre-Barthes: 192, 199, 200
© Cover of Lélia Gonzalez and Carlos Hasenbalg, *Lugar de negro* (Rio de Janeiro: Editora Marco Zero Limitada, 1982).

Colophon

Editors: Vanessa Grossman, Ciro Miguel
Design: Something Fantastic (Elena Schütz, Julian Schubert, Leonard Streich, with Fernanda Tellez Velasco)
Copyediting: Max Bach
Printing and binding: AS Printon, Tallinn
Typeface: Caslon
Paper: Holmen White 70g

Die Deutsche Bibliothek lists this publication in the Deutsche Nationalbibliographie. Detailed bibliographic data is available on the internet at www.dnb.de.

Ruby Press
Schönholzer Str. 11
10115 Berlin
Germany

www.ruby-press.com

ISBN 978-3-944074-39-9